COMFORT
IN
GRIEF

HOW TO SUCCESSFULLY NAVIGATE BEREAVEMENT

EDWARD KEEBLER

Comfort in Grief
How To Successfully Navigate Bereavement
by Edward Keebler

Copyright © 2023 by Edward Keebler

Paperback ISBN: 978-0-990326-2-1
Ebook ISBN: 978-0-990326-3-8
Hardcover ISBN 978-0-990326-4-5

Cover design by BespokeBookCovers.com

Contents

Foreword

My personal message to readers…

Grief is not a linear experience that can be accurately gauged by steps and phases. It's more akin to a wild mustang that bolts from the gate and all one can say is, "It went that way." Of course, there are many commonalities we all share in the loss of a loved one, but how does one combine the vigorous individuality of impact and expression with a method that effectively guides us through grief? That is the primary objective and focus of this book.

When I was a young father, my baby daughter, Jessica, died in my arms. Later in life my toddler son died while in the care of another person, and not too many years ago, my wife died. Needless to say, I have experienced significant loss in life as well as the accompanying grief. During my time of bereavement, the materials being touted as effective methods of processing the loss of a loved one were only slightly useful.

The mind of the newly bereaved is often in a fog where everyday activities and maintaining concentration is difficult. As such, stories are an effective method of occupying one's attention and retaining information. Former parishioners that I haven't seen in decades, say they still remember a certain story I told during a sermon. Most of us can easily recall the stories of "Noah and the Flood," "David and Goliath" or the "Woman at the Well." Jesus taught using stories with moral lessons. In the same manner, each chapter will begin with a story that introduces a topic. The instruction that follows will not contain complicated psychological jargon, but practical information related to the grieving process. In order to facilitate optimal retention, each chapter ends with a review of the chapter as well as tips on "Things to Know" and "Things to Do."

I also want you to write your own story. I'm not necessarily talking about a polished manuscript for publication—but at least some notes or bullet points. You will be asked to jot down and date your thoughts and emotions throughout the reading of this book. This process not only helps to solidify the content of the material but serves as a record of your growth. I've taught group grief classes for several years and encourage my attendees to take notes. Without exception, those who take notes are amazed at their growth and transformation after only a few months. Notes record growth, and one needs to be affirmed of growth and progress in the experience. Otherwise, you may feel stuck—like nothing is progressing and each day is the same repeated and painful existence.

Your writing can be recorded in a simple spiral notebook or in the accompanying, *Comfort in Grief Workbook*. The workbook contains additional data and research, along with more detailed writing guidelines. By the end of the book, you will have a record of your thoughts and feelings about all the material, and you will be able to look back and see tangible evidence of your growth. Most readers can consume the book's contents within a few hours; however long-lasting progress is better achieved by revisiting the book on a quarterly basis. Many of the people in my group grief class repeat the class two, three or even four times. Each time the material is revisited, new perspectives or insights are obtained because you will have advanced to a different point in the process.

All the stories in the book are true and based on real life experiences as viewed from my perspective. I have changed the names of many of the characters for the sake of their privacy. Some of the stories are humorous, some are inspiring, others are simply me, exposing my heart and vulnerability as a means to encourage you to do the same.

In my personal life, I have served the church in many capacities, from youth pastor to lead pastor, military chaplain, foreign missions, and currently as a hospice chaplain. I have officiated over 200 funerals/memorial services and provided thousands of hours of grief counseling. In my present position I serve as a hospice chaplain. I am bedside with terminally ill patients and their families, offering comfort and support as their loved one transitions into eternity. Some think hospice is tough, and it can be at times, as personal attachments come into play. Overall, I see myself as a doorman to heaven. I simply encourage and offer support as lives transition from here to eternity.

My prayer for you is that you are inspired and encouraged by the contents of this book and that it will be a useful tool to guide you in the years to come.

Well wishes,
    Edward Keebler, M.Div., PhD

The Disclaimer...

The information contained in this book are the expressed opinions of the author and should not be perceived as personal advice or therapy. Any actions taken by readers after exposure to this material are due to the sole discretion of the individual consumer. One may want to consider seeking the counsel of a local pastor or a licensed therapists who specializes in grief recovery.

Chapter 1
Who Is God To You?

The death of a loved one is always a surprise, even when it's expected...

I was a young minister when I first experienced death on a personal level. I came home for lunch on an impulse to spend a few minutes with my wife and children. We had two beautiful, healthy girls and my wife Anne was eight months pregnant with our third child. As soon as the girls saw me, they assumed it was playtime. My three-year-old met me in the doorway, attaching herself to my leg with a hug, and sliding into a sitting position on the top of my shoe. Her two-year-old sister followed, saddling up on the other. I walked Frankenstein-style, wearing my girls as boots, until I became tired and slowly sank to the carpet. We called what followed "wrestling." More accurately it was the two of them using me as a human jungle gym and climbing on me, but it was always fun. After our bonding time, Anne greeted me with a kiss and hug.

She slowly deposited herself into the soft cushions on the sofa, attempting to discover a comfortable position while balancing the added weight and girth of her pregnancy. This was no easy task. Today, she wore a pair of white maternity pants, and I noticed a quarter-sized red spot between her legs. Obviously unaware of the spot, I brought it to her attention, and she retreated to the bathroom. Moments later I heard her screaming and at that point I realized something had gone horribly wrong. I don't remember Anne ever screaming before… ever. "I'm bleeding! Call the doctor! Blood is gushing out of me!"

I frantically dialed the number to our OB/GYN and was on the phone with her within a minute. She was the mother of one of my seminary friends and eager to offer assistance. I doubt she would have risked offering the same advice for too many others; "Eddy, wrap towels around her, get her in the car and take her to the hospital immediately! Do not wait for an ambulance!"

While Anne gathered and tied towels around herself, I swooped the girls into my arms and ran next door. My neighbor was a member of our congregation and destined to be home at that moment. I'm usually very calm but was barely able to stutter my emergency situation and must have said something nonsensical. She instinctively knew I was in trouble and gladly received our little ones, who would be picked up by their grandma later in the day.

By the time I got to Anne, she was already inside our car with the passenger seat reclined to a near level position. Under normal circumstances, I am a relatively safe driver, but I found myself speeding and desirous of a magic button that would provide me with warp speed. I felt slightly conflicted each time I passed a speed limit sign that boldly proclaimed the maximum allowed speed as being 65 mph. Under the circumstances, perhaps I should have been easier on myself. I'm sure the folks in the congregation would be okay with me attempting land speed records if they knew the reason. Just when I thought I was over the temporary guilt, I noticed that I was rapidly approaching a California Highway Patrolman. The officer seemed content driving at the posted speed limit. I did slow down a little and looked at him but his mind reading skills must not have been functioning as well as I had hoped. He quickly accelerated, pulled next to me, and put his hands out as if to ask, "What are you doing?"

I pointed down to Anne, but she was reclining so low that the officer could not see her. In a near comical motion, he glided his hand over the police star prominently displayed on the door of his cruiser like a model demonstrating a product. I felt as though he was saying, "Did you not notice that this is a police car and that I'm a cop?"

He appeared to be a real nice man and quite understanding, but he soon insisted that I pull over. I shook my head "no" in an exaggerated motion from side-to-side while pointing to Anne who was, in his mind, no more than an invisible friend. He responded with an equally assertive up-and-down head motion and pointed to the side of the road.

Initially, I didn't want to alarm Anne as to our speed or the fact that we were now involved in a police chase. Lacking a solution, however, I looked down at my wife and calmly asked, "Anne, wave at the police officer."

Her voice was weak but filled with surprise. "There's a police officer? Why is there a police officer?"

She raised her hand above the bottom edge of the window and in view for the officer to see. With raised eyebrows, I glided my hand over Anne and then toward the officer as if to say, "See? I'm not crazy. There's a real person here."

It was at this point that the officer ended our once friendly dialogue. His expression changed and his motion became clear that he wanted me to immediately pull over. I mouthed the words, "I'm sorry" and shook my head "No." He pulled behind me and followed for several miles with his emergency lights flashing. Finally, a directional sign appeared indicating the turn off for the hospital. It was only a mile away. The highway patrol car continued to follow behind me in a chase position, but the officer obviously radioed ahead for backup. By the time I reached the end of the off ramp, a roadblock was set up. I could only turn one direction and that was into the hospital emergency area. Two additional police units were there waiting for me. When I stopped the car at the entrance to the emergency room, two hospital staff members were positioned at the curb, waiting for us with a gurney. Before they could attend to Anne, the police had to make sure the crazy driver of the economy car was contained. Up to this moment, I had never had a gun pointed in my direction. It produces an immediate level of fear and discomfort. From behind I heard the officer talking to me over a loudspeaker, "Put your hands out the window!"

I've had a couple of moving violations during my years of driving, but I've never been ordered to put my hands out the window, especially with guns pointed at me. I had no idea they expected me to put both hands out the same window. I assumed they wanted one hand out of each window. The driver's side was easy, and I nailed it on the first try. The problem came as I attempted to stretch my wingspan across the length of the entire front seat and place my right hand out of the passenger window. By the time I stretched that far, I noticed my left hand disappeared back inside the vehicle. The command kept coming from the loud-speaker, "Put BOTH hands outside the window!"

As hard as I tried, my arms weren't long enough to cover the distance between both windows. In the end, I stuck my left arm out the driver-side window and waved the other around inside the car. I was desperately hoping this was not a pass-fail test because I was not eager to be shot for being stupid.

Glancing up at the rear-view mirror, I saw the officers laughing at something and then holstering their guns. The medical team quickly moved in to take Anne. By this time the blood had completely saturated the towels and she was obviously very weak. I was relieved knowing that she was being attended to and that she was safe. Whatever price I had to pay at this point, it was worth it.

The officer approached my window and calmly asked me for my license. I found it difficult to look at him. I'm not sure if it was guilt or shame or the fact that I disrespected him by disobeying his authority. I exited the vehicle when he asked me—and finally summoned enough courage to look up at him for the first time. He was a tall, middle-aged African American man with a moustache and kind face. He asked me a series of questions and I was certain it was leading up to me being handcuffed and taken away to jail. I told him everything I knew and experienced earlier in the day, beginning with the blood spot and up to the time I passed him on the freeway.

He told me if I were ever pulled over again, and asked to put both hands out of the car, it's easier to put them both out of the same window. I was a little embarrassed by my obvious error but told him I felt lucky not to have been shot. With that said, he handed my driver's license back to me and walked away. All the police cars left at the same time, and I stood there for a full minute in shock. I wasn't even cited for speeding. I was never able to thank this man for his understanding and graciousness. If by any chance, sir, you ever read these words, thank you.

By the time I parked the car and caught up with Anne, her situation had taken a turn for the worse. The medical team administered several tests but couldn't stop the hemorrhaging—her life was now in danger. As with the deliveries of my first two children, I was there to witness the birth of our newest child. But there was a notable difference in the delivery room with this experience. The physicians were very serious-minded, and I could tell from the way they looked at me that something was terribly wrong. It didn't take long for the test results to come back and confirm what the doctors suspected. The fetus was alive at the moment, but the baby had a multiplicity of medical issues, all of which were potentially fatal. I was told that if the baby were to survive the birthing process at all, he or she would likely not live through the day. Within minutes, I heard a faint cry. The nursing staff cleaned and bundled up our baby girl and then placed her on Anne's chest. Tears streamed down my wife's face and all I could do was squeeze her hand. I felt helpless, realizing her pain was far greater than mine. She had carried the baby for eight months and bonded with her while I was meeting our newborn for the first time at this moment. Words were not sufficient for the heaviness of the room. I held Anne's hand until the medical team escorted me to a seat in the nursery. My daughter, now clean and bundled, was placed in my arms and I held her for about an hour before the doctor came in with more shocking news. My wife, Anne, had only a fifty-fifty chance of surviving the night.

I looked into the cherub face of the baby in my arms and prayed. It wasn't my first prayer of the afternoon—I had been talking to God throughout the day. My communications to God weren't the more polished and refined prayers I offered from the pulpit, they were quick bursts of thoughts and mutterings, mostly comprised of pleas for help and divine intervention. They were nearly thoughtless and instinctual, but at the same time, honest and filled with the frailty of my humanity. *"God help this car not to fall apart at this speed... God don't let any cops or parishioners see me driving this fast... God keep Anne and our baby safe... God don't let the police shoot me."*

My newborn daughter had dark hair and beautiful features. Judging by her physical appearance alone, one could easily assume she was a normal, healthy child. Both Anne and I agreed on a name and determined if the baby was a girl, we would call her Jessica, which means "grace." In the months leading up to this day, Anne and I developed a nighttime routine with our two girls. The four of us gathered on our bed before going to sleep and talked to Jessica. Our three-year-old, Angela, was intrigued with the ever-expanding size of mommy's tummy and the motions the baby made as she kicked in the womb. She was fascinated by the notion of a growing baby in mommy's tummy and was very vocal about wanting a new brother. It seems she was a little disgruntled about having a two-year-old sister who would take her toys. In her mind, having another sister would only complicate an already bad situation. Nicole, our two-year-old, was not mature enough to process too much of the information but was happy to be on the bed with the rest of the family. Anne had a nice singing voice, so she and the two girls sang together. Music isn't my gift, so I told jokes and tickled her big sisters to make them laugh. I'm sure Jessica was familiar with our voices, even in the womb. Back at the hospital, I sporadically talked to Jessica for the next couple of hours until she peacefully died in my arms.

A brief time later, Anne was out of surgery, but I wasn't able to see her. She was heavily sedated, and her situation remained very critical. It was now early evening, and the stress of the day was beginning to catch up with me. The physician who worked on Anne told me she wouldn't be able to talk to anyone until at least the next day. The best thing I could do was to go home and rest, and come back early in the morning. It seemed like sound advice, but I was conflicted with the thought of leaving Anne alone. What if she became conscious and I wasn't there, or worse, what if she died in the night and I let her die alone? I stayed until late evening and was never allowed to get any closer to her than the waiting room, so I left.

The house was dark and strangely quiet when I walked in. It is in a moment such as this that one realizes and cherishes those oft taken-for-granted memories of family. Only hours earlier in the day I was walking across the room, wearing my daughters on my feet as boots and holding my wife in my arms. In virtually an instant, everything had changed. My very predictable, routine life had been turned upside down; Jessica died in my arms and now, Anne may not make it through the night. I could not help but think—to ponder at length, the possibility of having to raise my daughters alone. I wasn't sure if I could do it without Anne or what life would be like without her. In a busy home with small children, moments of silence are cherished because they seem rare. But now, standing in complete silence, I yearned for nothing more than to hear the clanging of toys and the sound of their sweet voices. I dreaded going to bed alone.

I arrived at the hospital very early the next morning only to discover Anne's mom was there before me. I could tell in a glance from her facial expression that Anne was okay. Anne's mom was a woman of faith and appeared unmoved by the circumstances. My daughters peeled away from her and greeted me with the usual news of their lives, playing show-and-tell with the small toys that grandma had given them. I can't remember ever listening as intently and enjoying the minuscule details of their stories as much as I did in that moment. The reality of death has that effect. I had become so preoccupied in pursuing the opportunities and challenges of life that I had nearly lost contact with the beauty and precious moments of life. Standing alone in a darkened room made me realize what transcends death are the everyday moments that are etched into our memories. What in life is greater than a three-year-old saying "I love you" to her dad? Does anything smell sweeter than a freshly bathed baby? Is there any sound that compares to the giggle of child, or anything that feels better than when they wrap their little arms around you?

Anne was still very weak when I saw her. I was astonished to think that women still died during childbirth—it never seemed like a possibility until today. The physician said it was not very common but that it did happen. Anne had come dangerously close, but she was okay now and was expected to make a full recovery. I greeted her with a kiss and sat next to her, holding her hand. She was swimming in grief, and I sensed it. I knew she was going through the normal grieving process, and I needed to assure her that it was okay. It's healthy to grieve and it doesn't display a lack of faith in God.

Anne's stay in the hospital would extend for another day or two before she would be released and return home. I teasingly reminded her about my poor cooking skills and how I was collecting fast food coupons to prevent us from starving. Knowing how out of place I am in the kitchen made Anne laugh. That's what I needed from her —to know that she was okay, and her laugh reassured me. Our attention turned to our three-year-old, Angela. What would we tell her? She was expecting a new baby to come home with us. How could we explain death to a three-year-old? I was usually tasked with the serious talks, so when Anne asked how "we" were going to explain, that meant me.

I waited until Anne returned home before I had "the talk" with Angela. I knew it was going to be a very brief time before my eldest daughter started looking around the house for the new baby we had so frequently talked about. I put Angela on my lap and told her that I had something I needed to tell her. I didn't have anything scripted —I thought a simple, heart-felt explanation would probably be best. I started by asking her where Jesus lived? She likes games and I suppose this felt like a game to her at first. She smiled, pointed to the sky, "In Heaven!"

Angela had practically been born in church, so she probably knew as much about Christianity as anyone her age. She understood that Jesus lives in Heaven and that He loves all the children of the world. The near boundless imagination of a three-year-old places no limits of what they can perceive Heaven to be. I'm sure in her little mind, Heaven was a beautiful and glorious place where she could stay up as late as she wanted and none of the little sisters took toys from their big sisters.

The difficulty of our conversation became evident when the word "death" was introduced. I asked Angela where we go when we die. My attempt was for her to make the logical leap and connect the dots to understand that when we die, we go to be with a loving Jesus in a very happy place. She put her head down and became somewhat bashful. She didn't know or couldn't piece it together in her mind. I was obviously asking for too much, so I gave her the answer. "Heaven is where we go when we die. It's a very happy place filled with love, and we get to stay there with Jesus forever."

Angela provided me with only a slight, ambivalent nod in response. I then told her that Baby Jessica was very sick when she was in mommy's tummy and that a few hours after she was born, she died. Angela looked up at me with an inquisitive expression. I stroked her hair and told her not to worry though because Baby Jessica was in Heaven with Jesus and was very happy. There was a pause but no response, so I prodded her a little, "Do you have any questions?"

She looked up me, her big blue eyes filled with innocence, "Can I go outside and play now?"

After she climbed down from my lap and scampered outside, I watched her play in the yard for several minutes. To me, she seemed to be her usual self. She wasn't sad or gloomy and appeared to be the normal, carefree, and happy child she ordinarily was. Anne called me from the bedroom, "How did it go?"

I flashed a big smile while laughing, "I think I'm a genius."

Knowing better, Anne displayed an unconvincing smile and continued to prod, "So how did she react?"

"I told her about Heaven, love, and Jesus and she seemed to get it. She's outside playing and seems perfectly happy. I must be the best father in the world."

Anne laughed. As I sat next to her on the bed I explained further, "Well, maybe not the best father in the world, but seriously in the top ten."

She laughed again.

A couple of weeks passed, and I came home to discover Angela playing in the front of the house. Rather than immediately entering the gate in my normal fashion, I stood outside and watched her play. The four-foot-tall hedge that surrounded the yard hid me from her view and allowed me to admire her from a short distance. She was engaged in a rather amusing game, tossing her doll into the air, and catching it... repeatedly tossing and catching. After repeating this activity for a couple of minutes, I could see that the object of the game was to toss the toy as high into the air as possible. After a few meager attempts, I could see she was determined to break some sort of doll tossing record by lowering herself close to the ground and extending her release. She was obviously encouraged by this new, more effective technique. It was now time for a world record attempt. She bent low to the ground, her hands carefully balancing the toy baby's weight, and then with a mighty grunt she shot upwards while releasing the doll at its highest point. In the process of making this record-breaking toss, she tumbled over backwards on the lawn, causing her to lose visual contact with her toy. By the time she gathered herself together, she had no idea that the doll's trajectory had placed it out of her view and on top of the tall hedge next to where I was standing. My initial response was to reach up and retrieve the doll for her, but I was far too entertained by her reaction. She bent over, looking all around the ground for the doll. When she didn't find it, she stepped back away from the house and looked up to the roof. Not seeing it there, she peeked around the side of the house; again, nothing. With her frustration mounting, she cupped her hand over her brow and began to look into the sky. It wasn't there either. Exasperated, she put her hands up in the air and said, "Well, I guess Jesus got another one!"

It was at this point I realized I had to forfeit my self-proclaimed "World's Greatest Dad" award. Despite my bold claims to Anne that I had effectively communicated the concepts of death, eternity, and a loving God to a three-year-old, I had done quite the opposite. I knew my daughter needed and deserved an answer, but my attempt was comparable to emptying a gallon jug into a sewing thimble. I failed in my attempt to portray a loving God and a wonderous environment as Angela understood Jesus to be nothing more than a baby snatcher that lived in the sky. Perhaps there was a lesson in the experience for me as well.

The Process

Grief is not a linear progression visualized in a straight line from point A to point B. It's also not something that can be confined within a neatly organized series of steps or phases—it's a squiggly line that begins at the moment of loss and continues until our last breath. Your squiggly line is unique to you, perhaps with some similarities to others, but entirely different from anyone else's path. Your journey of grief cannot be confined, only directed. In the end, if one makes small but deliberate movements in the prescribed direction, the result is peace.

Grief is a journey. At present, simply getting out of bed may be difficult and dragging oneself into the shower may be considered a good day. As stated in the Forward to the book, each new subject and chapter will begin with a story. The simple reason for this is that within the swirling, emotionally entangled and grieving mind, it's difficult to absorb detail and instruction. Stories have a way of capturing the emotions and speaking to our hearts, even when our minds are numb or disconnected by pain. But my story is my story. Of course, you may be able to relate to my story, but my desire is to direct you into unraveling your own story. I am aware that this seems impossible to those experiencing a recent loss, but please bear with me. You have a story to tell, and your story will serve as a measure of progress and guide you through the pain of grief.

Many experience erratic sleep and wake up exhausted, having suffered several bad dreams. We are in a state of shock and disbelief so waking up in this state only places us back in a similar nightmare that still doesn't feel real. In general, many feel numb, and we find ourselves wrestling with such issues as anger, guilt, sadness and loneliness. Some of us feel physical aches and pains, fatigue, loss of appetite, brain fog, helplessness and a loss of hope.

Whatever basket of maladies one carries, grief recovery is a series of small steps and many failures. You must commit to the process and in your own time, you will be able to look back and acknowledge how much you have grown and improved. It is common for us to continue wrestling with acute pain and several ancillary issues months into the process, but looking back, you'll be in a much better state than when the journey began. The months that follow will consistently be even better.

For those who desire a deeper look into each topic, an accompanying workbook is available for a more in-depth examination of each subject and chapter. The workbook will provide the reader with additional material, resources, exercises and space to journal or record thoughts and responses. Although being exposed to the material will be extremely beneficial, the journey of grief still lies ahead, and the necessary work remains unfinished. There are no shortcuts in this journey but there is a process that leads to resolution.

Your Story Begins Here

Who is God to you? This chapter is not an apologetic defense of faith or an intellectual debate over the existence of God, it's but a simple question as to the presence and priority of God in your personal life. When one faces the devastating loss of a loved one, it often results in a crushing reexamination of our decisions and values. It's common for people who are hurting to become angry with God, to feel betrayed, abandoned or unfairly judged. *Why God? Why did you allow this to happen? Are you even there? Do you even care?* For now, at this place in our grief journey, we are not going to attempt to answer these questions, but only to acknowledge them. At this point, a theological formula to satisfy the mind may appear trite and will do little to mend the heart and soul. For now, all you can ask of yourself is to simply express the emotions of grief. Yell at God if you feel inclined—allow yourself to be angry, upset, defeated, and disappointed in Him. God can handle your grief and all the accompanying emotions. Allow yourself to be raw, real, and vulnerable. It's okay to feel weak and defeated. Acknowledge your wounds and begin the healing process by taking small steps forward. When you fail, and you will indeed fail, wipe your slate clean, and start again the next day by taking a small step in the right direction.

The story of Angela and her dolls displays how easy it is to misunderstand the concept and nature of God. As we progress in our journey, visualizing our growth helps us to understand the progress we've made from confusion to clarity. It's important that you record your present emotional state because you want to be able to look back and see your measurable growth. It's comparable to a child whose parents measure their height on a door frame each year. Journalling your experience is a very good start. Begin with a date and simply convey your thoughts, experiences, challenges, and emotions. If this is difficult, simply provide a date and simple bullet points. The more effort one puts into recovery, the more benefit will be received.

Review

Who is God to you? It's okay to express your brokenness in honesty. God understands and embraces us in our times of anger and despair. Grief inhibits our spirituality, and it may be difficult to feel God's presence, but His promise is to never leave us or forsake us. In this time of personal darkness, we may lash out at God but it's okay to doubt, be angry and question God. Your journey of grief is unique to you, but your recovery is contingent upon your effort in the process.

Three Things You Need to Know

1. *Grief is unique to the individual.* Several contributing factors determine how we express grief including gender, race, age, ethnicity, faith, coping style, personality, life experience and even the manner of death. Siblings will grieve differently for the loss of the same parent and parents will grieve differently over the loss of a child.

Some are very demonstrative in expressing grief while others feel grief as deeply but express it in silence. Others deflect grief with humor. The point is, don't allow anyone to define your expression of grief or put you in a box of their expectations. Grieve as you see fit and refrain from criticizing others who don't grieve like you, or share the same emotional experience as you.

2. Grief is an emotion, bereavement is a process, mourning usually refers to burial rites and rituals. Many times, these terms are interchanged with little consequence.

3. *Grief is an emotion,* so it is subject to radical swings of expression. One may feel wonderful for the first time in days and be in tears minutes later. Bereavement is a slow and steady plodding of the course.

Three Things to Do

1. *Talk to God.* You're probably feeling hurt, angry, disappointed, or betrayed by God. Tell God whatever you're feeling, no matter the emotion.

2. *Take a daily bath or shower* and maintain your normal hygiene and grooming.

3. *Write something down.* Start with the date and simply record what you're thinking and feeling on this day. Write a prayer, poem, scripture, or complaint—and if you have something you're grateful for that day, write that down too. Be real, not religious. Express your emotions. Begin recording your successful journey of grief.

> *"Weeping may stay for the night, but rejoicing comes in the morning."*
>
> — Psalm 30:5

Chapter 2
Dreams

I was a little surprised by the number of people who attended Jessica's funeral. We only expected a small group of immediate family and close friends to be present for the midweek ceremony, but many others had come. No one knew Jessica apart from Anne's swollen womb, so it was easy to conclude that those gathered for the service were there to support Anne and me. I think many people made a connection to Jessica's young, abbreviated life and it was amplified by the visual of her two toddler sisters standing at graveside. Many remarked as to how wonderful the funeral was, but I don't recall much of it. Anne was still experiencing abdominal pain and I was preoccupied with concerns about her physical and emotional condition. Our toddler daughters were surrounded by all the people who loved them and as such, were remarkably content. I came away from the experience only remembering many of the faces and emotions of the ceremony. Everything else was a blur.

Once home, Anne and I returned to our normal busy routines. Hectic days were little more than a distraction from having to deal with our unspoken grief. My heartache was realized more by observing Anne's pain as she internalized her sorrow. On one occasion, while in the process of seating and securing our two girls in the backseat of the car, I saw her reach her hand out behind her as though waiting for Jessica to hold it. It didn't matter that Jessica was a newborn and couldn't have possibly have been able to extend a hand for her mother—grief often sways from the path of logic. When Anne felt no response, she turned around to search for our missing child who wasn't there. Upon realizing what she had done, Anne took her place in the front passenger seat and quietly sobbed.

Evening meals produced another challenge. On the days Anne set the table, she occasionally and inadvertently set an extra plate for Jessica at the dinner table. Our normal nighttime routine of giving the girls a kiss and hug before bed was disrupted as she frequently paused at the door as though she had forgotten something. Many of our once fluid activities seemed oddly incomplete. I didn't ever know what to say to Anne or if there was anything I could say to make things better. Invariably, each situation ended with me holding her until she slowly drifted from my embrace.

Not too many weeks after the funeral, our day ended in the usual manner. With the girls tucked in bed and asleep, Anne and I spent a few minutes together before retiring to bed ourselves. As far as days go, it was more routine than memorable, but that would soon change. Aside from kissing Anne goodnight, I have no further conscious memory of what happened next, so I must have quickly fallen asleep. Most of my dreams are random and abstract; they're a series of rapidly changing scenes filled with odd situations and surreal environments. I rarely remember the minutiae of these intangible images. But this dream was distinctly different in that it was not random, and I remembered every detail. It followed a flowing chronology and when I woke up, I felt as though I had been in the presence of God. This was a singular event and unlike any I had experienced before or since.

My dream began with a drifting sensation. Within this dream state, I was entirely aware that I had died but my heart and mind were completely at peace. The manner of my death and the details of my former existence were entirely inconsequential, and I was not plagued by even the slightest amount of fear. It didn't matter that I couldn't feel my feet touching a solid surface, that everything appeared to be a cloudy gray or that I really couldn't see anything of distinction. My most identifiable emotion was curiosity. I felt at peace, secure and unthreatened in this environment but immediately became aware of a soft and alluring musical melody playing at some distance away from me. It was a single instrument, maybe a flute or clarinet, perhaps neither. The tune was sweet to my ear, unavoidably enticing and I felt compelled to discover the origin of this fabulous music as it seemed to possess more than simply an audio quality.

Distance was difficult to measure because in the dream it was not an obstacle. My motion was determined by my thoughts and will so if I desired to move to a certain location, I had only to think it so. I saw a bright light and moved in that direction. As I glided toward the fringe of the light, details and colors became more vivid and the musical tune became more distinct. I was conscious of the fact that the light was so bright it would have been impossible to look upon with mortal eyes, yet I was able to stare directly into it without pain or discomfort. Time was nearly impossible to gauge but it felt as though I was at the fringe of the light for only a moment before noticing a figure emerging from the brilliance. At first all I could see was an outline but as I neared, I could see that it was a little girl who was approximately ten years old. She was standing in a field with what appeared to be rolling hills of flowers —millions of beautiful flowers that at first sight, resembled the background of an impressionist painting. Her facial and bodily features were the only objects in clear focus as the flowered hills behind her were obscured by the brilliance of the light surrounding her.

As our eyes met, I felt as though I was being bathed in love— gentle waves at first and then I could feel it flowing through me, around me, and inside me. It originated from the little girl that I now recognized to be my daughter, Jessica. She was a beautiful child with long dark hair and possessing familiar family features. She was clothed in a sheer white garment that resembled the shape of a choir robe with flowing sleeves. We began to communicate, but it was without words and far beyond telepathy—a language I can only describe as perfect communication. We exchanged not only data but emotion, motivation, and purpose as I understood everything she expressed as well as she knew it in her own heart and mind. I knew that she too, understood my deepest thoughts and emotions. Most importantly, everything communicated between us was enveloped in love and was absent of judgment, condemnation, guilt, or remorse. Oddly, I never touched her. Apparently, there was no need as the maximum level of intimacy was achieved without physical contact.

I was not entirely conscious of time, but I became aware that our personal exchange was coming to an end. I became curious once again but was confident something else was to follow. Jessica smiled, lifted her right arm, and extended it to her side as though introducing me to someone or something. She slowly moved her arm from side to rear. As her hand leisurely swept over the rolling hills surrounding her, my eyes were opened to the backdrop, and I was able to see it with the same clarity in which I saw her. A new world was revealed in colors, shades and hues that were beyond anything I previously understood. What I first thought to be vast fields of flowers, were actually people. I could see them clearly now and aside from their massive number, each had his or her own distinct musical tone. Whether expressed vocally or instrumentally, they all blended perfectly with one another. As Jessica's hand glided over the enormous gathering, I could identify individuals and groups of people as their unique voice or instrument chimed into the growing choir and symphony. They were the saints of Heaven who had come to greet me and welcome me into Heaven. This song began as a sweet, soft, and alluring note, a single drop that cascaded into a deluge of wonderment and sound. I raised my arms, engulfed within the shower of sensations—colors, sights, sounds and emotions that were infinitely beyond my human experience.

I woke up from the dream with tears rolling down my face, still tingling with the emotion and sensation of experiencing something otherworldly. I could feel the presence of God and wasn't initially sure if I was on Earth or in Heaven. Only seconds later the familiar objects of our bedroom came into focus and I realized what I experienced was a dream. With my heart still racing, I went over each part of it in my mind because I did not want to forget a single detail.

I allowed myself a few minutes to calm down and then gently stroked Anne's shoulder until she awoke. Although a little disoriented and not immediately happy about being awakened in the middle of the night, she sensed the matter was important. Normally we talk about issues in the morning when our minds are fresh, so this was a departure from our norm. Anne took a few minutes, and then sat up in bed and gave me her full attention. I relayed the details of the dream to her with unusual animation and conviction. By the time I finished with all of the details, Anne covered her face with her hands and wept. It was a good cry, one of relief and gratitude. From that moment on, her heart seemed to be satisfied. She never again set an extra plate on the table or reached for the hand of a third child. She was reassured that Jessica was in Heaven and grateful for the confirmation we received in the dream. We think of Jessica many times throughout the year, especially on her birthday, but it's no longer a painful thought. In our minds we can see the beautiful young girl who will greet us at our passing and introduce us to those who have gone before us.

The history of the Christian faith is conveyed in dreams as they are cited from Genesis to Revelation. Some serve as warnings, others communicate a promise, future event, encouragement, instruction, or judgment. There is no certainty that a grieving individual will receive a divinely inspired dream of their loved one basking in heavenly glory. I will take the point a step further and admit that such dreams are uncommon.

Every normal person dreams, even though most dreams are abstract, confusing, and quickly dissipate from memory. Immediately after experiencing a devastating loss, one is faced with a barrage of new stresses and challenges that frequently disrupts routines and leads to a lack of sleep. It's not unusual for the newly bereaved to live within a weary fog, simply attempting to sustain themselves moment-to-moment and day-to-day. Sleep can become a sought-after refuge that allows us to rest our hearts and minds from reality and the unrelenting bombardment of pain. Denial from heartbreak is a fleeting escape that can only survive in sleep. After a fitful night of attempted slumber, in one's first waking moment, it's not uncommon to extend a forgetful hand to the cold side of the bed. Others may open doors to empty rooms or call out the names of the recently departed. The silence and renewed awareness of our loss and aloneness crashes down on us while our souls scream in agony. For some, it may feel like our hearts are going to burst within us and even screams offer no relief. There are still others who are more accepting of the situation but continue to yearn for and miss the physical presence of their loved one. All of our experiences are uniquely our own. Furthermore, our expression of grief is unique for each loss, and members of the same family will express grief in their unique manner for the same person.

Grief can be so overwhelming it cannot be constrained to our waking hours, and the shock or numbness can spill over into our sleep. In the days and weeks following the loss of someone we love, dreams tend to be erratic. Some refer to such experiences as grief dreams, bereavement dreams or visitation dreams. Regardless of the descriptive label, these dreams are connected to one's loss and occur after the death of our loved one. Bereavement dreams allow those experiencing grief the opportunity to connect with the reality of their loss in incremental dosages, sometimes reviewing the loss while at other times, offering a connection to the departed. What we see and experience in our dreams is not real, but the emotions attached to these experiences certainly can be. In essence, dreams help to process our hurtful experiences with our emotions and memories.

Review

It is common for those who have lost a loved one to experience vivid dreams. The content of a dream may be the result of something as simple as the byproduct of a meal or an emotional venting of tragic circumstances. At times, God speaks to us in dreams and a large portion of the Bible is comprised of dreams or responses to a dream. Historically, every culture in recorded history has held dreams with high regard for insight and spiritual direction. Dream interpretations can be effectively used as a tool for inspiration and encouragement, but a prudent person will seek God and wise counsel before implementing a direction indicated in a dream.

Things to Know

*Always review and implement the previous suggested, "Things to Know" and "Things to Do" from the previous chapters. Continue to add to your story.

1. *One may not remember many details of a funeral* or the events immediately following the death of a loved one. You're likely still numb, in a state of shock and enveloped in a sort of emotional fog and disbelief. You may not weep at the funeral. It's not due to a lack of love, it's primarily because the situation doesn't yet seem real. Don't be critical of other family members if they don't grieve like you do. Everyone's grief process is unique.

2. *The departure of a loved one from our lives does not erase their presence from our hearts and minds.* It's not uncommon to forget that the person we love has passed. One may think they heard them talking in the next room or even see a glimpse of the person. You're not crazy. Most people have similar experiences.

3. *Dreams are normal and healthy.* They help to connect our emotions and experiences in sleep, assisting the grieving person in processing the seemingly unbearable loss we are experiencing. Even unpleasant dreams can be beneficial by forcing us to deal with unresolved issues. At times, God speaks to us in dreams. At other times, dreams can be useful tools for creative ideas and inspiration. Some find benefit in recording their dreams and keeping a journal of them.

Things to Do

1. *Keep a voice recorder or writing material next to your bed* and keep track of the details of your dreams.
2. *Read* a daily devotional, the Bible—something encouraging each day.
3. *Take a walk, go outside, let God speak to you apart from the structure and busyness of life.* This is not a suggestion to battle a blizzard or hurricane winds, but find a place and time where you can see and experience God in nature.

> *"You are never too old to set another goal or to dream a new dream."*
>
> — C. S. Lewis

Chapter 3
The Journey Of Grief

Funny Bike Story

I had just become acclimated to the fact that I was middle-aged when almost out of nowhere I began to receive unsolicited correspondence from AARP and other organizations that cater to senior citizens. Senior citizen? That's a moniker for old people, isn't it? I'm not old. Well, sort of not old anyway. Admittedly, I do enjoy the discounts at the movies and at some fast-food restaurants but even when I ask for the discount, secretly inside I feel like I'm scamming them. Really, I'm not that old. Scientists claim that men my age only produce ten percent of the testosterone they once produced in their youth. They must be wrong! My ego hasn't diminished with age, so the testosterone must be there too, right? Male logic doesn't necessarily have to be fact based; it only has to fit the scenario. Perhaps completing a long-distance bike ride was the evidence I need to deal with this notion of growing old.

I woke up before my alarm, ate a very light breakfast and arrived at the Oceanside Pier in time to see the eastern horizon began to glow with the light of a new day. By the time I lined up with over 2,000 other riders in the 50-mile, "Bike the Coast" event, visibility was excellent. Those near me in line were very chatty and notably excited. There was a racing team from Italy, another from France and me... go team Lakeside.

We were released in waves to avoid congesting the public road-ways. The wait provided me the opportunity to dialogue with several riders. Those I spoke with were very polite, but I noted their consistent downward glances. I knew my fly wasn't down because it took considerable effort to squeeze my frame into padded riding shorts. This garment comes with no plan of escape and no fly. For a guy, it's like wearing Spanx with a couple of women's hygiene products stuffed into the bottom. It's not a pretty site but fifty miles of familiarly with a bicycle seat shaped like the nose of a dolphin demands drastic measures. Not that I'm old, but I do understand that with age, anal sphincters weaken and the last thing I need to worry about is being penetrated by a bicycle seat at mile thirty-eight.

No, their downward glances had nothing to do with my fly, it was my bike. It's obviously a trail bike and judging from the rest of the crowd, only one of a handful at the event. They were very polite —overly polite, but looking back, I think they were trying to warn me or at least give me a heads up. One twenty-something guy spoke to me with a concerned look. "Umm, sir..." (why do they all call me 'sir'? I'm not that old) "Sir, what kind of bike do you have there? What's the gear ratio?"

I was in line for less than five minutes. The event had not even started, and I was already being called out as a novice. What else could I say or do? I came clean and confessed like a good Christian, "Yeah, this is my first biking event... like, ever. I don't know anything about gear ratios. Until nine months ago, I hadn't ridden a bike since about age twelve."

The young man looked at his girlfriend who jumped into the conversation, "Do you have any electrolytes or energy candy? What kind of fluid do you have?"

I thought to myself, electrolytes? energy candy? What were these people talking about? In desperation to correctly answer at least one question I blurted out, "I have water!" The couple looked at one another again and then looked away, almost in horror. I couldn't tell —was it because they were embarrassed for me or that they knew I was doomed and they couldn't bear to watch. That had to be it. I was a cadaver on wheels to them.

My wave departed and I found myself riding with a gregarious IT guy from Northern California. He stayed in a hotel near Poway the night before and pronounced the name of the city with a long "o" as in police. I knew straight away he wasn't a local boy, but I did enjoy his company for the first six or seven miles. About then is when we entered into the first stretch of hills, and when I began to reflect on why the young man was asking me about gear ratios. As I ascended the most difficult part of the hill, I tried to find a lower gear and there was none. I found myself huffing and puffing up the small incline like the character in the childhood story about a little locomotive, "I think I can, I think I can." All the while, everyone was passing me by.

"On your left… on your left," seemed to be the phrase of the day as I hugged as closely to the road's edge as possible. My fellow travelers were not just passing me, they were gracefully cutting through the wind like the nearby seagulls patrolling the beach. Their fancy road bikes didn't clatter and cling during gear changes —they seemed to glide. They hummed past me, enjoying the view, with no sweat and at twice my speed.

The first major hill was physically demanding, but the second was psychologically demoralizing. I must have reeked of desperation. The people were so kind, but every other person seemed to look over and say, "Sir, are you okay?" If I had the breath, I would have told them not to call me sir, because I'm not that old. As it was, the best I could do was muster a nod that I was fine. I really wasn't fine because I was beginning to realize that I still had forty miles to go. I finally understood what females mean when they say they're fine. When it takes more energy to explain something than finish it yourself or having to admit to the obvious, being fine is the less taxing alternative.

By the third hill I must have appeared so obviously tormented that people stopped asking if I was okay. Instead, they looked at me like a physician who was forced to inform a patient of a terminal prognosis, "Sir, do you need any electrolytes? Energy candy?" I dare not admit to ignorance on top of everything else, so I remained silent and dispelled my potential rescuers with a friendly sway of my head. At this point, I still didn't know what electrolytes were, but if they provided me with some superpower, I was ready to stop at the next market and pick some up.

I honestly thought I would never make it to the halfway point and rest stop. One of the local bike shops provided an array of cut bananas, orange slices, trail mix and icy sticks. I was seriously considering taking my free snacks and going home but I'd still have to ride twenty-five miles to get back to my car. The temperature was over ninety degrees by now and I overheard people saying the route was really fifty-two miles, not fifty. To my good fortune, while nearly passed out against a shaded wall, I met Gabby and her friend Leanne. It took Gabby all of thirty seconds before she offered me a cube of chalky substance containing electrolytes. After I consumed it, she handed me a packet of energy candy and told me to take the whole pack. She and her delightful British friend watched as I downed the magic formula. I didn't immediately feel better, but the duo seemed so intent on helping me that I felt obligated not to let them down. After we rested the three of us set out together. The first hill on the way back was like a slow death but the two ladies were right there with me, not giving me the opportunity to quit. I made the first hill, then the second and was finally over the most difficult part of the return route. I never saw them again after that, but I know I wouldn't have made it without them.

At about the forty-mile mark, my stomach began to gurgle and I realized I probably needed a restroom break as soon as I crossed the finish line. I'm not sure if it was the heat—which was now pushing the mid-nineties—or the snacks, electrolytes, or the bag of energy candy, but something wasn't right. I was now facing a new challenge. In addition to having little strength left in my legs, each bump in the road represented a knock on a door I didn't want to open.

The directional signs pointed off the main roads and back down toward the pier. Less than two agonizing miles remained. I was confident I was going to make it at this point, but I wasn't sure as to my condition. The road turned down to the beach bike path and I could see the finish line only a half mile away. I tried going faster and sprint to the finish line but I didn't have the strength. The photographers awaited us at the finish line, and I had originally intended to raise my hands and smile. At the last second, I concluded that the risk was too great and if I lifted my arms I would somehow relinquish what little control I had left of my sphincter. I didn't want my finish line photo to display a frantic, wide-eyed look while mouthing the word, "Oops!"

I coasted across the finish line, perhaps with a grimace on my face, but I made it. I was pretty beat up, lightheaded and glowing with a sunburn. My hands displayed an odd tan line in that my fingers, from the knuckles to the fingertips (the part of the hand tucked under the handlebars) were significantly lighter than the rest of my hand. My hair was matted to my head but even after removing my helmet, it felt as though I was wearing it for several hours afterward. On the drive home I found it difficult to break away from being in "bike mode." Subconsciously I sped up on the downhill portions of the freeway as a means to use the inertia for the next incline. Once home, I intended to lie down for only five minutes before taking a shower. I woke up four hours later, cleaned up and satisfied my rare craving for a chocolate shake. Would I do it again? Maybe when I get old… but not with a trail bike.

It's okay to laugh. Laugh as often and as vigorously as you're able to, because the tears are not far behind. Take respite from your pain whenever the opportunity avails. As odd as it may seem, my "Funny Bike Story" serves as an allegory for our grief journey. Processing grief is like riding a bike? Everyone knows how to do it? The simple answer is, "No." One can elect to make the same mistakes I made in my fifty-two-mile near death experience or, learn a few simple techniques to avoid that pitfall.

The following are lessons illustrated from the *Funny Bike Story.* This does not to serve as a paradigm for grief recovery but does provide parallels to important insights.

- *It's okay to laugh.* Dispel the thought that you're dishonoring your loved one with laughter. I have officiated over two hundred funerals and memorial services and it's rare when laughter is not evident during a ceremony. A loved one is not honored with self-imposed suffering. Enjoy life when you're able to, and don't allow yourself to feel guilty when you do. Ignore those who judge from a distance.

I've served the church in several capacities in my lifetime, i.e., from a youth pastor to a lead pastor in the civilian church, military chaplain, foreign missions, and now as a hospice chaplain. One of my hospice visits brought me bedside to a Marine with end stage Parkinson's Disease. He had no mobility and was unable to communicate aside from facial expressions and limited speech. In order to speak he had to take a deep breath and exhale the words. Next to his bed was a photo of himself in uniform, standing with his arm around his pretty wife. The picture depicted a tall, muscular man who had attained the highest enlisted rank—Sergeant Major. His rank and decorations displayed a lifetime of impressive achievements. As he lay in bed, his stiff body appeared as though he was at attention—only his eyes tracked me as I entered the room. I picked up the photo on the bedside table and held it as I turned back to him. "Is this you?" He nodded in the affirmative.

"I'm an ex-Army Chaplain. You're a Marine?"

He inhaled deeply and with his eyes still fixed on me, "Oorah!"

I smiled and teased him, "Sergeant Major, you couldn't get in the Army?"

The good sergeant rolled his eyes and laughed. It was probably the first time he had laughed in a very long time. On a follow-up visit with another patient, I happened to see his wife in passing. She came up to me and asked if I was the chaplain who made her husband laugh and she thanked me. The Sergeant Major passed a couple of days later.

- *Know the route, obstacles, resources, and your capabilities.* The second parallel in the bike ride analogy is to avoid being naïve and assuming one is already familiar with the subject (especially men). As a novice, I signed up for a bike ride not knowing the terrain, equipped with the wrong kind of bike and ignorant of gear ratios or what my bike's capabilities were. I was not aware of the physical strain the ride would have on my body and I lacked the proper provisions, thus I was ill prepared to take on the challenges of the route.

When approaching the subject of grief recovery, it's beneficial to know the route. You do not have to be an expert as there are helpful resources available for free or at a low cost that will guide you through the process. One can participate in grief recovery groups or, if you prefer and have the resources, spend time with a counselor who specializes in grief recovery. Immediately after experiencing a loss, it's difficult to get through a day but having a map outlining the process will be an enormous benefit. If you only have the strength to take a small step each day, make sure it's a step in the right direction.

Take care of your body. After losing a loved one, a prudent step to take would be to get a medical examination to assess problems or challenges. It's always beneficial to eat well, exercise and maintain social contacts. As a caution, we can't try to solve one problem with another problem. Some people compensate for their loss by discontinuing to eat, while others feed their sadness with excessive consumption. Food, alcohol and drugs (including prescription medications) are never a healthy solution for grief recovery.

- *Ask for help when you need it.* I would have never finished my bike ride without the assistance of others. Leanne and Gabby provided me with the electrolytes and energy candy my body needed plus, most importantly, they provided the encouragement I needed to finish the trip. They were total strangers who came out of nowhere to help me. The duo began bike riding and entering long-distance rides as a means to lose weight. Remember, superheroes don't always wear capes. Out of all the fabulously conditioned athletes at the rest stop, it was these two who saw my need and responded. When we are at a place of need in our life, allow God to choose and send whomever He chooses to knock on your door. Frequently, those we thought we could count on the most will abandon us, and sometimes strangers will show up to become our source of strength.

It's not uncommon for the grieving to arrive late to church and leave early, or to skip church altogether. I did this myself. I became weary of talking about what had happened and having to explain details to everyone who considered me a friend. I became tired of the sad eyes and the way people looked at me. I retreated from church people in a vain effort to be treated as a normal person—but I wasn't normal, and people could sense it. I attempted to isolate myself, but then I began to crave contact and a hug from a friend. As C.S. Lewis stated during a period of grief, *"I see people, as they approach me, trying to make up their minds whether they'll 'say something about it' or not. I hate if they do, and if they don't."*

In the end, the solution for me was to be around others who shared my experience and suffered loss as well. I volunteered to lead a grief recovery group at a local church for seven years. Those who adjusted best and lived the highest quality lives were those who established relationships within the group and continued to love, nurture, and encourage one another after the class had ended. One group developed their own fellowship and continue to meet to this day.

- *Is what you're feeling real?* Once the bike ride was completed, I felt the effects of the event for days to follow. Even with my helmet removed, it felt as though it was still atop the matted hair on my head. In my mind and logic, it was obvious that if I was holding my helmet in hand, it couldn't possibly be on my head. But it felt like it was. On the drive home I found myself speeding up on the downhill portions of the road to take advantage of the inertia to climb the next rise. Again, the experience was not real, but merely residual energy from my past experience. In a time of great loss, many of the things we initially perceive as real, are not. If the assumption is not challenged, what is not real becomes fear. Fear is a monster we will face in an upcoming chapter.

Steps, Phases, Statistics and Diagrams

After my daughter died and before I had the vivid dream, I sought solutions in an assortment of books and theories on grief recovery. At my present point in life, I better understand their value but immediately after experiencing a loss, I couldn't make sense of the material. I could never figure out which step or phase I was in at the moment—if I was repeating a previous step or if I was progressing at all. There were days when I felt as though I was examining my steps of grief like a daily horoscope. This is why I prefer simplicity. The grieving mind, especially when one's loss is new, is often numb. I like the perspective provided by Patricia Garfield, PhD, as she explains the journey of grief as consisting of three basic parts. I have summarized her work into the following:

- Numbness: characterized by shock and sometimes denial of the death. Things seem unreal and one's mind can be in a fog.
- Disorganization: marked by emotional chaos, anxiety, fear, depression, and guilt. Some feel as though they are

going crazy, and others go into a state of shock that may result in a long-term emotional paralysis.

• Reorganization: when one develops new roles, skills and relationships while adjusting to a new life.

Another great resource is the work of William Worden, PhD. Worden dispenses with steps and phases altogether by stipulating that grief recovery can be reduced to four simple tasks—a "to do list" of sorts. In other words, don't worry about where you are on a grief chart, simply do this along the way. I think this is a wonderful perspective.

Here are Worden's four tasks of grief:

1. Accept the reality of one's loss.
2. Express emotions, work through the pain of grief.
3. Adjust to a new environment, a life without the loved one.
4. Relocate emotions from painful thoughts to pleasant memories and move ahead with life.

The grieving mind is disorganized, and any kind of list may appear unrelated or confusing at the moment, but mark these pages as you'll want to refer back to them at a future point. The content of this chapter will provide you with an overview of the journey that lies ahead. In the upcoming chapters, we'll discuss potential obstacles to your progress and how to identify and avoid them.

Review

We started this journey with the question of where God resides in your experience of loss. This was not a theological question or an apologetic response but a simple query to yourself. *Who is God to you and how has your loss impacted that relationship?* We then examined the subject of dreams. The content of the dream chapter was not only to explain the nuances of dreams following the loss of a loved one, but to stir thoughts of an afterlife. *Where do we go when we die?* Having introduced these two topics, we set out on our journey of grief recovery with a broad overview of where we're going. In this chapter the *Funny Bike Story* was used as an analogy to depict what lies ahead in our grief journey and how to prepare for it. This was further enhanced by Garfield's three parts of grief and Worden's four tasks, or "To Do List" for grief.

Things to Know

*Always review and implement the previously suggested, "Things to Know" and "Things to Do" from the earlier chapters. Continue to add to your story. Keep writing, making notes and dating them.

1. *Expressions of grief.* Depending on your personality and expression of grief, some common emotional responses to grief are weeping, weariness, sleeping in excess, insomnia, numbness, brain fog, forgetfulness, disorganization, helplessness, relief, becoming reclusive, untidy, overeating, not eating, increasing the consumption of alcohol or medications, headaches, body aches, nausea, displacement of time and several others. Chances are, if you're doing something now that you weren't doing before, it's related to your grief. It will pass, unless you choose to make it a habit.
2. *You're not crazy*, even if you feel like you're losing your mind. Your world is upside-down, and you can feel like a stranger in your own home, but this is normal and will eventually go away.
3. *Most often, grief doesn't require medical intervention.*

Things to Do

1. *Join a group for grief recovery* and get to know others who are going through the same experience as you. Support groups sessions are very beneficial when you're ready to expose your grief to others.

2. *Express your creative side.* Take an art class and learn to dance, draw, paint, write, sculpt or create.

3. *Don't be afraid to ask for help.* You may be overwhelmed and the responsibly of the world has fallen in your lap. Don't suffer alone and in silence.

> *"To truly laugh, you must be able to take your pain and play with it."*

— Charlie Chaplin

Chapter 4
Celebrating Life And Memories

A few years after Jessica's death, I entered the military chaplaincy and was assigned to an installation located near a national cemetery. As part of our normal responsibilities as military clergy, it was common for us to conduct funerals for deceased members of the armed forces. Because of our proximity to the national cemetery, I've officiated scores of funerals, largely for veterans who served their country with honor and distinction. In addition to the decade of service I had as a civilian pastor prior to this, I was also trained in military protocol and understood the order and formality of the military ceremony. The difficult part was learning how to adequately respond to the surviving family members before and after the ceremony as it was an entirely different skill, only learned as a result of personal study and experience.

Chaplain Barnes, my senior chaplain, was sitting in his office when I returned from my first funeral. He must have seen the distress on my face. Out of obvious concern for me, he looked up from his desk and asked, "How did it go?"

I assured him that we had served the veteran's family well and that the funeral had been completed with positive input from those in attendance. Chaplain Barnes remained silent as he intuitively knew there was more to the story. After some hesitation I finally blurted out the real issue. "How do you deal with the hurt? I had no problem with the order of the ceremony or delivering the message, but how do you look into the faces of the bereaved without feeling their pain? I can't help but feel some of their grief."

Chaplain Barnes was a highly regarded clergyman and a competent officer with over twenty years of experience. He had been conducting military funerals a lot longer than I, and he impressed me as being someone who knew all the ropes. Due to the number of funerals that chaplains were required to officiate at this installation, we were frequently and repeatedly exposed to the bereaved. As such, most chaplains were reassigned after an abbreviated tour of duty. Chaplain Barnes had been at this post a lot longer than most, but he seemed to have discovered a way to emotionally survive the situation. When he invited me to observe his next funeral, I eagerly accepted.

The wait for the next ceremony was brief as my senior chaplain was scheduled for a funeral the following day. Dressed in our Class A uniforms, comprised of a military suit and tie, we drove to the cemetery together. Rather than stop at the facility's front office where the family of the deceased was gathered, we went directly to the staging area. There we met with the military honors detail that was tasked for funeral that day. Depending on the rank of the service member and additional family requests, there are some variations of protocol. The troops assigned this day were comprised of the normal assembly of pall bearers, a firing party, and a bugler. Although the participation of the color guard in the service is relatively simple, their military precision and professional presentation contribute greatly to the overall impact of the ceremony.

I quietly stood aside as Chaplain Barnes confirmed the particulars of the service with the detail leader in charge. Once the family was seated, the ceremony began, and the entire event lasted all of fifteen to twenty minutes. It was a flawless procedure in that the color guard delivered the flag-draped casket to the staging area, their salutes were perfect, the rifle volley rang out over the gravesite, "Taps" was played, and the American flag was tightly folded and handed to the grieving widow with a memorized line of condolence. When Chaplain Barnes finished, he walked up to me with a smile and remarked, "That's how it's done."

I cannot be critical of Chaplain Barnes's method. He was much more experienced and had been at this assignment much longer than I. Perhaps what I observed was simply his technique of protecting his heart from being nibbled away until he had nothing left to give. I do not judge him for his choice of method because his ceremony was flawless. But I know in my heart, he purposely insulated himself from the grieving families and their pain as a means of self-preservation. I wrestled with his method in my mind for the next day or two. In the end, I concluded that after my experience with the death of my daughter, I could not conduct a ceremony that placed precision over heart and formality over genuineness. I made the conscious decision that from that moment on, I would risk emotional injury to display compassion to the grieving families. I could not limit my exposure to their grief as though it were a fatal disease, even though I knew I risked emotional consequences over time.

My next funeral, booked for Master Sergeant Michael James Monroe, was scheduled only days later. I asked the funeral director to have the family meet with me forty-five minutes before the ceremony and to provide me with an office so that I could introduce myself to them. When the day of the funeral arrived, the mildly bewildered family ambled into the office looking as confused as the funeral director. After I introduced myself, I sat with a half dozen members of the immediate family including the mother of the deceased, his surviving spouse and their four adult children. I explained to them that I was assigned to conduct the ceremony but lacking a relationship with their loved one, I wanted to spend time with them to learn some of the details of his life. I already had in my possession the veteran's full name, date of birth and other pertinent information. Regardless, I initially asked the family for much of the same information to facilitate a more candid dialog and transition into a deeper exchange of their personal experiences. With the simple questions out of the way, I asked, "What was your loved one's most admirable quality?" Opinions varied because he uniquely impacted everyone's life in different way, but each verbalized quality was greeted with nods of affirmation and a smile or chuckle from the others.

Once I felt the family opening up to me, I asked them to tell me one of their favorite stories about Sergeant Monroe. Courtney, the third-born daughter, spoke up immediately. She told a story about an automobile accident that occurred when she was first learning to drive, and the incident resulted in her crashing her mother's new car. Mom's head snapped back in astonishment as the rest of the siblings contributed a hearty laugh. Courtney quickly blurted a rapid-paced and wide-eyed confession to her mother, "I made him promise he would never tell you, mom!" Courtney and her mother laughed together while wiping their tears away. It was a promise her dad had obviously taken to the grave with him. That was the kind of response I wanted from them. I didn't want to bury a man and reduce his life to a list of medals and awards he had earned as a soldier. Of course, his military service was an important part of his life but the individual that existed beyond the battlefield and warrior persona was the life he lived as a man of faith, a son, husband, father, and friend. I wanted to know that person.

I asked a few more questions and listened to several more stories. It all led up to the final question. "Tell me about a negative quality your family member displayed and how you recall it being demonstrated." An outsider may think this to be a risky question and it probably was, but by this point in the interview everyone was freely talking, laughing, and crying together. Many of the family secrets were now out in the open.

Sergeant Monroe's wife of thirty years was the first to speak. Her gravelly voice was soft but firm. "He was the most stubborn man I ever knew." I had to wait until her adult children stopped laughing before I could hear her explanation. "He wanted a blue dress shirt to match his favorite new tie and I found one on sale and bought it for him. According to my husband, Michael, it wasn't the right shade of blue. I told him it's the same shade as the blue on his tie. He never even took the shirt out of the packaging. That shirt must be fifteen years old by now. I almost had him buried in that shirt."

The eldest son, Zach, chimed in and added a story about how his dad decided to pull his own tooth. "He had a molar that was bothering him, but dad hated going to the dentist. One day he must have had an 'invincible warrior' moment and decided the tooth had caused him enough pain. He went into the garage, took a pair of rusty pliers, and yanked the tooth out himself. I remember him walking into the house with a swollen face that got worse and worse throughout the day. After a couple of hours, his face was nearly twice normal size. He took a couple of Motrin, the Army cure all for everything that ails you, and went to bed. It kept getting worse so the afternoon of the following day, we had a family intervention and called one of his buddies over to force him to see the dentist. He could have died from the infection but despite all the pain, he still seemed proud that he pulled his own tooth."

I jotted down the necessary notes and comments, and then excused myself to meet the military detail leader at the staging area. The family followed closely behind, and the ceremony began as usual. After the doors of the hearse were opened, the color guard took possession of the casket, blanketed it with the Stars and Stripes, and marched it into the staging area. Per protocol, I stood at attention and saluted as the flag-draped coffin passed me. With everyone in position, standing under the cover of the staging area, I removed my hat and approached the podium. Most often at this point, the bereaved are distracted and still experiencing shock, often looking down or aimlessly staring away. With the reality of their loss staring them in the face, they are undergoing somewhat of an out-of-body experience. Their physical bodies are there but their hearts and minds are often crushed in despair. It was different today.

I looked to the first row where the family was seated and noted their demeanor. They focused their attention on me through eyes glossed with tears and restrained smiles. On the family's behalf, I acknowledged and thanked those in attendance and began the ceremony by stating the deceased's full name, Michael James Monroe. His biography was written in the bulletin that was passed out to those in attendance, but I felt it necessary to verbalize and honor his most significant achievements, among them Master Sergeant in the United States Army, recipient of the Bronze Star, devoted husband, father, son, soldier and friend. With the necessary accolades spoken, I introduced those to the human being that we had gathered to show due honor and respect. Few knew that he had kept his daughter's secret of crashing her mother's car for all these years. Those who knew Sergeant Monroe weren't surprised as they nodded and smiled with approval. After a couple of additional personal stories, those in attendance freely laughed and shed tears along with the family. I enjoy funerals where laughter is permissible, and lives are celebrated with good memories. The biggest responses were from the stories that demonstrated Sergeant Monroe's loyalty, honor and especially his stubbornness. Like the rest of us, Sergeant Monroe was a deeply respected but perfectly flawed human being. He will be missed by those who love him and genuinely value him for the fine brush strokes of his life.

The service could have ended at this point, and I think everyone would have left feeling content, but I had yet to cover the best part. This life that we have on earth is only the beginning of what is to come. Jesus said, "I am the resurrection and the life. Those who believe in me will live, even though they die; and whoever lives by believing in me will never die."

The afterlife is a mystery to us because as humans, we consistently rely on our day-to-day experiences and physical senses for survival. When Jesus rose from the grave and was standing in front of the disciples, Thomas would not believe until he saw the nail prints. Addressing Thomas, Jesus said, "Because you have seen me, you have believed; blessed are those who have not seen and yet have believed." The Bible states that, "...faith is being sure of what we hope for and certain of what we do not see." This same faith in Jesus Christ is the cornerstone of eternity. One cannot grasp the wonderment of an afterlife or conceptualize the reality of Heaven without faith. Faith, however, does not imply a lack of intelligent thought or an avoidance of factual evidence. Faith is not a manufactured emotion, or a state of mind based on wishful thinking and psychological desperation. Faith is a heartfelt response to the life and message of the historical figure, Jesus Christ. Faith is examining the factual evidence of Jesus's death, burial and resurrection and coming to conclude that He is in fact, God incarnate and the savior of humanity.

In order to put flesh to the bones of the message, I told the story of Jessica's death and the subsequent dream I had. It was not an attempt to equate the quality or duration of two vastly different and separate lives, but to identify with their feeling of loss. Beyond that, it was to demonstrate that heaven is real. God is real. There is nothing more comforting than to know that our lives do not end in disappointment and grief, but we will live on in eternity with a loving God and surrounded by the people of faith we know and loved on earth.

My final words to those gathered were taken from John 14:2, "In My Father's house there are many dwelling places; if it were not so, I would have told you. I go to prepare a place for you." Jesus spoke these words near the end of His life on Earth. He understood the disciples and their concern about their future apart from Him. Jesus was assuring His followers that His words were true and that their place in Heaven was secure for all of eternity.

Looking into the eyes of the family members, I stated with assurance, "When your final day comes and as a believer, you are ushered into the afterlife, I have little doubt that Sergeant Monroe will be there to greet each of you into God's kingdom. Based on the stories I heard of him, he may even be wearing a blue shirt."

I took a step back from the podium and placed my cover or hat back on my head. This is the signal for the detail leader to bring all participating military personnel to "present arms" or to salute. No matter how many funerals I preside over, and even knowing the moment when it comes, I recoil from the first round of the rifle volley. The three loud shots from seven riflemen ring out over the grave as a symbolic reminder of the military tradition to clear the dead from the battlefield. As a Christian, I like to think of the three volleys in terms of Father, Son, and Holy Spirit.

At the conclusion of the rifle volley, "Taps" is played by a lone bugler. The familiar tune never seems to lose its impact. The mournful melody triggers a flood of emotions as we are reminded, one final time, a soldier has fallen. This is our final goodbye, our last farewell. In my mind, I imagine the soldier, sailor, marine or airman giving one final salute to those present and turning to pass on into eternity.

The Stars and Stripes that drape the casket are carefully folded, each turn representing a part of military history, tradition, and faith. The folds honor mother, father, women and faithfulness to God and country. The eleventh fold represents Judaism, the twelfth Christianity and the final fold displays a field of stars representing one nation under God. After the final fold, the loose ends are tightly tucked in, forming a neatly shaped triangle. The military service member at the head of the casket receives the flag, crossing their arms over it and pressing it to their heart. The flag was then passed to me. I held the Stars and Stripes over my heart as I marched to a point facing Sergeant Monroe's widow. I paused, and then with one hand on top and the other on the bottom of the flag, I bent over and placed Old Glory into the hands of his widow with the words, "On behalf of the President of the United States, the United States Army and a grateful Nation, please accept this flag as a symbol of our appreciation for your loved one's honorable and faithful service."

It is not uncommon for the next-of-kin's hands to shake as he or she receives the flag and most often, holds it close to their heart. As Sergeant Monroe's widow kissed and shed tears upon this cherished symbol, I stood at attention and saluted one final time. Unlike other military salutes, this is a prolonged salute that is reserved for the fallen soldier. It is deliberately slow as a display of respect and almost feels like a reluctant goodbye. With the salute complete, the service is over.

Yes, it hurts to officiate a ceremony this way. The fallen soldier is not just another casualty but a person whose life had meaning and significance. Under different circumstances he could have been a member of my congregation or even my friend. As seen through his family's eyes, I value his sense of humor, his sense of loyalty and I admire him as a person of faith, a soldier, family man and generous friend.

———

The importance of mourning…

Although mourning is often used synonymously with grief, it refers more to the process rather than the emotion of loss. This process is usually demonstrated in a manner consistent with the social and cultural norms to publicly proclaim the loss of a loved one. The life that once was, is now deceased, and the ceremonial display commemorates this to other family members, friends, and the public. Our loved one is dead.

The importance of mourning rituals is that they help the grieving to accept the reality of one's loss. In the great majority of instances, one cannot effectively grieve or initiate the bereavement process until the reality of their loss is acknowledged and accepted. This is an adaptive process that occurs over time as one confronts their situation in a state of emotional vulnerability. The goal is to develop a new but altered lifestyle without the deceased. In the end, we are able to, "emotionally relocate" (J. William Worden, *Grief Counseling and Grief Therapy*) from our loved one by retaining an endearing connection with them through memories, stories and events, but moving on to enjoy life and love again.

> *"The rituals of mourning help us to acknowledge the passing of a loved one and to publicly say goodbye. Many are numb and in an emotional fog. It's almost as if one is able to exist outside of their own body and watch the events unfold because nothing seems quite real. The temptation is to believe that any moment I'll awake from this horrible dream."*
>
> —J. William Worden

———

The process of adjusting…

In what is described by Margaret Stroebe and Henry Schut as "The Dual Process Model of Coping with Bereavement," an effective method of bereavement is achieved by oscillating between "letting go" and "holding on." The holding on is demonstrated by "loss-oriented" coping, which is realized by typical grief responses, i.e., reviewing media of our loved one, crying and yearning for their touch or presence. Letting go is a "restoration-orientated" coping mechanism that is experienced by having to deal with the secondary losses associated with the loss. Tasks such as the family finances, mowing the lawn, cooking or shared tasks are suddenly our sole responsibility. In the case of the loss of a child, it leaves a void of preparing meals, providing transportation, laundry, or social activities. Whatever "hole" the absence of our loved one leaves, we fill the void by engaging in a process that allows us to adequately express our grief while learning to adapt to the changed circumstances. At times we will be actively confronting our loss while other times we will seek relief by occupying our attention with other things, a subject to be addressed in greater detail in an upcoming chapter.

Adjustments...

For most of our marriage, Anne was a stay-at-home mom and loved her role as a wife and mother. Without her in my life, I suddenly became responsible of the household for my own self-preservation. I hated grocery shopping the most, especially the laundry detergent aisle. I'm not sure if it was the combined odor emanating from all the cleaning products or the thought that after I finished shopping and preparing my own meal that I had to launder my clothes. In the days immediately following Anne's death, the mere touch of a grocery cart handle nearly sent me into a panic. My fellow shoppers seemed way too content at this activity—taking their time, strolling down the aisles and examining each product as if they had all day to it. If someone smiled at me, I assumed they knew I was doing it wrong. In my haste to get out of the store, I frequently bought things I already had and some things I couldn't identify except by its label. Taking anything back was out of the question as I'd rather suffer the loss than return to the store and admit ignorance on top of it. I'm ashamed of some of the things I ate. I discovered that most things are tolerable when covered with peanut butter.

When Anne and I were dating in college, she used to make wonderful desserts and I assumed she was a great cook. Little did I know that desserts were the only thing she knew how to make. After we married, she volunteered to do the cooking and I was eager to agree to that deal. The first night we had cheeseburgers. I like cheeseburgers and was quite happy with that choice. The second night we had cheeseburgers. I wasn't sure why, but I like cheeseburgers. The third night we had cheeseburgers. As much as I like cheeseburgers I asked if we could have something different the following evening for dinner. That's when I found out desserts and cheeseburgers were the only food items she knew how to cook. We looked at one another and started laughing because she knew my cheeseburgers were not as good as hers.

Soon after, we were on the phone with my mom, and she asked if we had any hamburger meat. I opened the freezer door and explained that it looked as though we had a year's supply. Mom knew we had a crockpot, so a reasonable solution was to cook a simple meatloaf for the following night. It seemed like a good idea at the time but when dinner came around the following day, the substance inside the crockpot was in liquid form. I'm used to seeing mom's meatloaf as a solid substance, but I wasn't going to disappoint my new wife and I had two bowls of it. I had diarrhea for two days. When I was able to eat again, we had cheeseburgers.

In the months that followed Anne's death, I continued to grieve as I pushed a grocery cart through the store. I didn't have a knack for it, always seeming to pick the cart with only three functional wheels. It was as though the grocery store knew that I didn't belong there, and the malfunctioning wheel screamed that sentiment to all passersby. I was still sad, I still felt the loss, and I still hated the laundry detergent aisle. But I was also able to recall the early days of our marriage and that brought a smile and some comfort. I remember that we survived many sub-par and monotonous meals together, but in time Anne became a remarkable cook and it all worked out. It will all work out again.

Beauty in imperfection...

There's a wonderful scuba diving spot about a one-hour boat ride off the coast of Maui in the Hawaiian Islands. Our group had the good fortune of having as our boat captain a young woman who, during the academic year, was a doctoral student in the field of marine biology. When a whale and her cub broke the water's surface near us, she quickly identified it, providing us with its characteristics and explaining how unusual it was to see a whale this late in the season. She speculated that due to the female's advanced age, she may have had trouble giving birth or perhaps was separated or unable to keep up with the rest of the pod. When she completed her explanation, I asked her how she knew the whale was old and our boat captain's reasoning was rather simple. One fin displayed marks of a shark attack, other scars and blemishes testified as to net entanglements, collisions with boats and a long life in the ocean. Although I noticed the wounds, from my vantage point and what captured my attention, was the enormity and beauty of the immense creature as it seemed to playfully escort her cub out to sea. Grief is like that. It leaves a wound that testifies of an investment of oneself into the life of another. From a distance, however, the imperfection is easily dismissed when considering the overall beauty of the creature and the adventures of its life.

In Japanese culture there's a term I have come to cherish known as wabi sabi. When a valued piece of pottery is broken, rather than throw it out, it is pieced back together by adhering the broken pieces together with gold. In the end, it creates an even more impressive work of art. Wabi sabi is the practice of seeing beauty in imperfection—beauty in things broken or flawed. Grief is like that. It shatters our life into pieces, but God carefully reassembles the broken shards with gold and puts us back together again, even more beautiful than before.

Review

Grief is not an exercise in forgetting our loved ones, but carefully packaging memories and moving forward through life without their physical presence. The funeral or memorial service serves as a public statement that the person you loved is now deceased and is not coming back. Our love for them results in the pain of grief, but our recovery results in our ability to appreciate their contribution to our lives and move forward. We are somewhat broken by the loss, but not destroyed. God places the pieces back together, mending our brokenness with gold. In the end, it's possible to love more deeply, value life more intensely, appreciate cherished memories and create future dreams and happiness.

Things to Know

*Always review and implement the previously suggested, "Things to Know" and "Things to Do" from the earlier chapters. Continue to add to your story. Keep writing, making notes and dating them.

1. *Memories are the link that connect us to our deceased loved ones.* Bereavement is the process or journey one takes after losing a loved one. Grief is the emotional response. The success of one's effort in this journey is determined by how we transition from our identity with our loved one to an individual without them. One may lose a certain sense of self as a husband, wife, father, mother, sibling, or dear friend. In essence, we not only grieve the loss of our loved one but the identity we shared with them. Our departed loved ones will never occupy the place in our lives that they once did, the living must go on without them. Although grief may never entirely end, it does get better. Successful grief eliminates the sharpness of our

pain as we make the conscious choice to process and forgive all the deficits of their life while focusing on and honoring their life with the cherished memories we shared with them.

2. *Life on earth is brief but eternity is only one breath or a heartbeat away.* Psalm 39:4 states, "…each man's life is but a breath." The New Testament adds to this in James 4:14, "You are a mist that appears for a little while then vanishes." Ultimately, we will all die. For the Christian, however, we are promised in Rev. 21:4 "He will wipe away every tear from their eyes; and there will no longer be any death; there will no longer be any mourning, or crying, or pain; the first things have passed away."

3. *The departure of a loved one from our lives does not erase their presence from our hearts and minds.* It's not uncommon to forget that the person we love has passed. One may think they heard them talking in the next room or even see a glimpse of the person. You're not crazy. Most people have similar experiences.

Things to Do

1. *Preserve Memories.* Reorganize family photos and videos, make a list of your favorite memories and characteristics of your loved one.

2. *Consider an art project.* Make a blanket, quilt, or pillow from your loved one's clothing.

3. *Donate on behalf of your loved one.* Give a donation to a charity or church, fund a scholarship program, or plant a tree.

> *"The risk of love is loss, and the price of loss is grief. But the pain of grief is only a shadow when compared with the pain of never risking love."*
>
> — Hillary Stanton Zunin

Chapter 5
Establishing A New Direction

Church Softball Story

I searched the church grounds in all the obvious places with no success. My final hope was to check in the storage shed where the lawn mower, miscellaneous tools, and extra paint was stored. Finally, there it was, nestled between a stack of five-gallon paint buckets—the equipment bag for the church softball team. I was the new coach and it was not a position I asked for, but as the newly appointed staff pastor, it was a responsibility that seemed like a good idea at the time. I rummaged through the outdated equipment and the records for several of the previous seasons. It was apparent from the scorebooks and other data that our church team had been the perennial bottom dwellers of the league for at least a decade. Many of the games listed in the scorebook were marked "forfeit," which was a clear indication that the church was unable to get enough players on the field for a legitimate contest.

Our fast pitch church softball league was a unique organization. They had been around for at least a few decades, and the people from their respective churches seemed to all know one another.

Unlike many softball leagues that play their games to empty stands, the church-based fans showed up to support their teams. Some churches organized picnics prior to the games and others just liked to meet new people and mingle with other Christians. I'm sure younger singles were there to see if someone showed up that piqued their interest. But don't misunderstand the comradery and fellowship with a lack of competition. The games were highly aggressive and competitive. Even in church league, it's sometimes just as hard to lose against a team that smiles and says, "God bless you" after a game.

The league organization went by an honor system and required only a few rules be observed. Every player in the game had to attend church at least once during the week and while competing in the games they had to refrain from certain behaviors such as cursing, drinking alcohol and belligerent behavior. The reality is, the rules weren't too different from those posted by the city leagues or observed by other organizations. The church league officials were astute enough to realize that softball could be used as a tool to expose people to Christianity, so their goal was to maintain a mutually respectful environment while being welcoming to those who didn't regularly attend church. The big issue for me as the new coach was finding quality players who were willing to attend church.

Our first game of the season was still a few months away, but I organized a practice to see who would show up and to determine what kind of existing talent we had. As expected, about a half dozen players came. I became immediately alarmed as they stood across from one another to warm up their arms by throwing the ball back-and-forth to one another. This was not supposed to be either dangerous or an aerobic activity. When my players weren't throwing the balls over the heads of their intended targets, they were throwing the ball to the wrong teammate. Most of the practice was spent chasing balls because my players either lacked the ability to accurately throw a ball twenty-five feet or catch an object the size of a small grapefruit in their glove. For this group, softball was a high-risk sport.

The most notable player of this group was a kid named Spencer Pierce. Spencer was a great guy—a big-hearted high school senior with good grades and musical talent. Judging by his raw size of, 6'3" and 220 lbs., one might be tempted to think that he had promise as an athlete. But that wasn't Spencer at heart. He loved music, played in the school band, and was shaped more like an amusement park bear than a competitive athlete. He wore glasses so thick it made his eyes appear as tiny fish at the bottom of a small aquarium. When he ran, his ginger steps created an image of a moon walk in slow motion—his energy seemed to be more directed to liftoff than forward progress. All that aside, when he was up to bat, and during those rare moments when he actually connected with the ball, he hit it a mile. As a right-handed batter, he missed most pitches but those he connected with were driven deep into right field. Anyone familiar with baseball knows that a right-handed batter normally hits with strength to left field. I couldn't tell if Spencer had very slow reflexes or if he was having problems seeing the ball. If it was something I could coach him through, I felt as though he could be an excellent hitter.

We needed more players. Word went out to all the church members and one-by-one, I received a tip here and there that this person or another possessed some degree of athletic ability. One of our worship leaders approached me and mentioned that her husband, Greg, was really good but he had not attended church since the age of twelve. I called him up, admittedly not having high expectations. I always appreciate it when a loving spouse sees more Superman than Clark Kent in their loved one, but the level of talent is usually far less than described. I met with Greg at a local park. He was taller than average, thin, and had long, long limbs. My first impression was that he resembled a spider monkey. I would feel guilty putting this comment in print if not for the fact that he later became one of my close friends and an elder in the church. The tricks we played on one another over the years are worthy of another story.

After warming up our arms, Greg took a spot at third base, and

I hit some balls to him. Mindful of my experience with the guys at our first practice, I hit a few gentle rollers directly to him and he easily snatched them up. He seemed a little frustrated with the process and asked if I could hit the ball harder. I chucked inside and hit a hard liner to his left. He scooped it up without effort. I tested his range and smashed line drives to both sides. He made diving catches and wasn't afraid to get dirty in order to catch a ball. I usually play third base myself, but this guy was so good I was willing to give up my position and move to the outfield. I remember the smirk on the worship leader's face that Sunday. I didn't have to say a word as she said it for me, "I told you he was good."

In the weeks that followed word got out that we were assembling a pretty good team. One of our college aged girls had a boyfriend that played shortstop in high school and his buddy played first base. Another woman's husband struggled with alcoholism and stopped going to church years earlier, but he loved softball and was a very capable pitcher. In all, we gathered about fourteen players, which included the original six who were still developing as athletes.

The team practice that followed was entirely different than the first. Our original six players had stepped up their game by simply being around better players; the bar was raised, and they seemed more determined to fit in with the higher standard. There was no doubt that we had talent, but the question remained as to whether we had a team. At the end of practice, we gathered together, and I mentioned the rules. There were only a few and the first was that weekly church attendance was mandatory—no exceptions. The second rule was no player could criticize another player for making a mistake. Mistakes and failure are a huge part of athletic competition, and everyone makes them. Superior athletes are not the ones who seem not to make mistakes—such a person doesn't exist. The better players are those who, after making a mistake, can recover and perform at or beyond their normal level of performance. The other side of rule two was that we were to become mutually encouraging to one another, especially after someone made a mistake. In other words, rather than project disappointment in a teammate's error, we were going to express confidence in their ability and build them up. Rule three was simply an exception to rule two. As the coach, I allowed myself an out to be able to offer "constructive criticism" to a player that could not be construed as a violation of rule two. I did not want to risk negating the effectiveness of the rule by simply offering instruction or taking charge of a situation. As far as playing time, we could not guarantee that all fourteen players would see action every week, but I assured everyone that if they didn't play one week, they were guaranteed to play the week following.

We held a fund raiser or two before the season began and that provided our team with their first new hats and uniforms. We were making a statement: a new team, a new look and a new winning attitude. We announced our first game to the congregation and when the day of our first game arrived, we actually had fans there to watch us play. It's difficult to imagine how we felt when we lost. It was a close game, and we did many things right but not enough to win. One of our better players showed up for the game but he wasn't in church that week, so I didn't include him in the lineup. The opposing coach complimented us for putting together a good team and stated with confidence that we should win some games this year. It was a nice gesture, but we were eager to snap the decade-long losing season streak.

We had a good chance to win the following week too, but our best pitcher showed up reeking of alcohol and I couldn't let him play in that condition. I was admittedly a little discouraged. The rules were simple, they just had to work. By the following game, the guys were a little tense and it showed on the field. We made some early mistakes, and it culminated in a blatant error by an infielder and compounded by another player raking him over the coals. I immediately called time out and benched the critical player. This was the only time in my life I can ever remember being cheered on by the fans of the opposing team. The benched player slammed his glove down in the dugout and sat with arms crossed for several minutes, but he survived. On the field, something different was happening—we had suddenly discovered our team spirit. The players were talking and encouraging one another, and our entire dynamic changed. We won the game by a large margin and the benched player celebrated with us. I think the difference is that rules are just rules until they are taken to heart. Once the rules were demonstrated, we had a choice to either band together or quit.

The team's attitude was undergoing a radical transformation. We were winning more games and I was able to take a step back from my role as cheerleader and allow the guys to take over. They were positive, affirming, and encouraging one another. As more and more church fans came to support us, they too, caught onto our contagious and encouraging attitude. As each player fielded a ball or stepped up to bat, they were greeted with a chorus of affirmation. If they made a good play or got a hit, they were cheered and if they fell short, they received consoling remarks and the sting of their imperfection quickly dissipated.

With only two weeks left in the season we were in second place. We were scheduled to play the first-place team in the final game of the season but in order for us to have a chance at winning the league championship, they had to lose their next-to-last game. We had to stay focused on our own game that week because a loss would eliminate us from contention. As the final pitches of our own game were successfully played out, news from the other field reached us. The team that opposed the league leaders had played the game of their lives and won! We were now tied for first place and next week's game would determine the final standings. We lost our first game of the season to the same team, but we were a different group of players back then. In the initial weeks of the season we had talent but lacked continuity, confidence and spirit. We were at a place now where we were confident we could beat anyone.

The level of excitement for the game that week was notably high. Large groups of fans from both churches, plus those from the other churches had come to watch the final game of the season. Do you remember Spencer Pierce, the big high school musician that was part of the original six? His parents came to the game. They didn't even know he was on a softball team until a week ago. Our recovering alcoholic was sober, and his wife was in the stands along with our worship leader, the spider monkey's wife. Also in the stands were the girlfriends, spouses, children, and parents of all our other players. Placed on a table in the middle of the crowd were two shiny trophies that stood three feet high or more. One was for the winning team, the other for the most valuable player.

Our team did not play well. We did all the things that led us to a string of victories all season but whether it was nerves or a lack of confidence, we simply blew several opportunities and found ourselves down to our final out, behind by one run with two runners on base. The next batter was Spencer Pierce. I was in the coach's box on the third base side and immediately called a time out. Spencer had struck out twice earlier in the game and I had one of my seasoned players sitting on the bench ready to pinch hit. The crowd immediately became quiet as it was an obvious move. As I stepped out of the coach's box, I felt my heart pounding and knew there was something else at play here. Have you ever had a "God moment?" The only way I can define it is by describing it as a divine deviation from one's normal act, intention, speech, or behavior. One fully intends to do something one way, and usually that way is perfectly reasonable and normal but there's a "heart check" that inspires or motivates one to do something completely different. That's what happened to me. It was as though this moment was the culmination of the lessons for the entire season.

I fought off the urge and signaled for my pinch hitter. He put on his helmet, grabbed his bat and stood in the ready until I made the official substitution with the umpire. By the time I reached Spencer, he was standing with his head down and slouched over his bat like his girlfriend had just broken up with him. The umpire looked up at me waiting for me to utter the words for a substitution but by that time my "God moment" had taken root. Spencer continued to look at the ground as I spoke to him. "Spencer, do you know how I've been trying to correct your swing all season because you always hit the ball to right field?" Spencer nodded.

"I want you to forget everything I told you. I want you to hit the ball into right field, two or three feet fair—which is normal for you… score these runners and win this game."

Spencer didn't immediately respond. I think he was so certain to hear he was being taken out of the game that it took a moment for him to process the message. His head slowly turned toward me, "I get to bat?"

"Yes, hit the ball into right field and score these runners." I gave him a pat on the back and returned to the coach's box.

The crowd was in stunned silence for a moment until a small voice squeaked out, "Come on Spencer, you can do it!" Almost immediately the rest of the crowd and our players chimed in as well. As the volume of the crowd grew, Spencer stepped up to the plate, pushed his thick glasses snug against his face and stood ready for the first pitch. Strike one! The umpire raised his hand in a definitive motion to confirm the call over the crowd noise. Spencer's shoulders slumped and I knew his confidence was being tested. He took a quick glance back at me and I simply pointed to right field. He swung at the next pitch and missed. Strike two.

At this point I was beginning to doubt if my God moment ever happened at all. In my mind I was trying to formulate an explanation to my team as to why I did what I did. In a matter of seconds, I was creating a speech in my head about second place not being bad after going a decade without a win.

Spencer stepped up to the plate the third time, this time bouncing a little at the knees in an effort to remind himself to keep his knees bent. Apparently, some coaching did sink in. The third pitch seemed to be delivered in slow motion as the crowd nearly gasped in unison. Up two strikes and no balls, the opposing picture made a smart choice, delivering a low curve ball out of the strike zone and on the outside of the plate. It was not a good pitch to swing at—but that didn't deter Spencer who was determined not to watch another pitch pass him by. When a softball is hit solidly by an aluminum bat it generates a crisp "ping." As Spencer's bat swung through the air, the resulting sound was more akin to the sound a watermelon makes from being dropped from a second story window onto concrete… a sloppy, mushy sound. It was not pretty but

Spencer hit the ball and it was heading deep into right field. It was going to be close, but no one knew if the ball was going to land in fair territory until it hit the ground. Fair ball! The ball landed thee feet inside the line and out of the reach of the outfielder. Spencer lumbered around the bases and slid into third base headfirst. After feeling his hands touch the bag, he looked directly at me, his eyes excitedly darting around in his fishbowl glasses. He was safe, as the ball had yet to reach the infield and he really had no reason to slide at all. The game was over... we won!

Time passed and everyone's lives moved on. One of my last memories of Spencer was seeing him trying to stuff the large trophy for being the game's MVP into the back of his VW Bug. Looking back, it wasn't so much about winning as it was defining character. Our performance on the field solidified the priority of a team's spirit and created a bond that transcends awards. Who would have thought at the beginning of the season that our unlikely hero would be a somewhat clumsy high school musician. For Spencer and his parents, it created a lifetime memory. For Greg, our spider monkey third baseman, it evolved into a committed life of service to God. As for me, I eagerly await future "God moments." To be candid, they kind of scare me a little. Who knows? Maybe I'll end up writing a book on grief recovery someday.

If you reflect upon the three phases of grief proposed by Patricia Garfield, and the four tasks of grief presented by William Worden, how does this story apply? If you recall, Patricia Garfield's third and final stage of grief is *reconstruction* and William Worden's third task is to *adjust to a new environment*. Both thoughts deal with the same or similar issues in acknowledgement of the fact that we need to adapt and redirect our lives as we rebuild from the ashes. How do we do this?

Church Softball Story is another allegory that provides a model to successfully rebuild a broken life. To reiterate an earlier point, you will remember the Church Softball Story far longer than any of the details of this book. The hope is to integrate the lessons within the story to reinforce retention and application.

- *Take inventory.* This is the part of the story where I searched the church grounds for the records and equipment. By taking inventory of the records from past seasons, I was able to ascertain that the team had been perpetual bottom dwellers for many years. It was a harsh reality to face but it had to be acknowledged in order to implement changes.

Losing a loved one leaves huge gaps in our lives. Whether the loss is a spouse, sibling, parent, or child, we are often faced with a barrage of lingering administrative and relational issues. Whatever tasks your loved one was responsible for, may fall upon you to complete or continue. This leaves us with not only having to grieve their loss but face a mound of added responsibilities. Relationships change too. Friends who were once intwined in our lives, may retreat to the fringe of our social circle once the relationship changes. We may become the "third wheel" of a foursome or the now childless parent of a once shared activity or sport. These are referred to as secondary or ancillary losses.

- *Recognize weaknesses.* In the first practice with the team, there weren't enough players to field a team and those that did show were not skilled players.

This is where you discover your deceased spouse had a unique accounting system that made no sense to anyone else. It may be that you have a lot less money and a lot more debt. You don't have the specific knowledge, contacts, or skill level they possessed and now you don't know what to do. Your half of the relationship centered on other things and now you feel stuck and helpless. Parents whose lives are wrapped around a child's activities feel lost, they pick up the phone to call an adult child or sibling and realize they aren't there for us anymore.

- *Seek help.* After the first practice with the half dozen guys
  that showed up to play, I knew this was not a group that
  would be competitive. They were great kids, possessing
  wonderful qualities but none of them were athletes. In
  order to solve the problem, I had to look outside my
  immediate sphere of influence and seek help from
  others.

The grass is knee-deep, you're getting overdue bills in red
envelops and you don't know the password to pay online. There are
death benefits available, but you must fill out the forms and it's difficult—not so much that you don't know how, it's a matter of lacking
the desire. Sometimes planning the affairs of a lost loved one feels
like betrayal.

Seek help from others. It initially feels like you're imposing on
people but you're not. Churches, nonprofit groups, and neighbors
are eager to help. They are constantly looking for opportunities to
serve the community, even if you're not a member of their congregation or group. You'll be amazed as to how many people want to
help others just like you—if only they knew you needed help. Join a
local group grief support group for emotional support and additional resources.

- *Follow a plan.* Without a plan, the church softball team
  would have repeated its former pattern and resulted in a
  disjointed mess. The plan was simple—attend church
  once a week, be encouraging to others, and take
  corrections from the coach.

The birds-eye view is that at first, you're going to be numb and
not be able to do much of anything, then things are going to be very
disorganized and after that we're going to reorganize everything to
fit our new environment. Along the way we need to acknowledge
the passing of our loved one, express the emotions of our loss, adapt
to a new environment, and finally, relocate emotions from painful
thoughts to pleasant memories.

It's a simple plan but a lifetime journey. There is no high-speed lane for the process, only a slow and steady path filled with failures and growth. The two go together hand-in-hand.

- *Surround yourself with positive, encouraging people.* Even with new uniforms, a new look and more skilled players, we continued to lose our first two games of the season. We didn't begin to win until our attitudes changed and we began to encourage one another.

Here's an odd dynamic when it comes to friends and suffering the loss of a loved one. This is not always true but it's common for those whom you thought were your closest friends to abandon you in your time of bereavement. Most will not admit to it, but your loss is too much of a reminder that life can be fragile and short. It's difficult for such people to see you and not be reminded of the reality of losing someone they love. Others simply don't know how to respond to your loss and feel uncomfortable being around someone experiencing such grief. In contrast, there are those who can relate to your pain and want nothing more than to help you in some capacity. Accept this kind of help and surround yourself with caring, nurturing and encouraging people. As a word of caution, do not rely heavily on any one person or you will burn them out.

- *Be open to God's voice.* In the final moments of the game, I wanted to ignore the gut feeling and any thoughts that entered my mind, especially at such a crucial moment in the competition. I thought I had it all figured out. I even tried to deny that God was speaking to my heart at all.

During times of intense grief, it's often difficult to hear God's voice. The surest way to hear God's voice is to read the Bible because it accurately portrays His words. But God also speaks to us in nature, in solitude, through others and in circumstances. I know a couple of people who state they have heard God speak to them in an audible voice. It's difficult for me to relate to that because it's never happened to me, but who am I to put God in a box? Most often, when people say, "God told me…" they are describing a feeling they received in their heart or spirit. I am a little leery of church people who begin every conversation with the "God told me" phrase but I obviously believe it happens. I believe that for those who walk a consistent life of faith, it happens often. What makes the softball game communication unusual is that my mind was entirely focused on trying to win the game. In my mind, I had everything figured out and didn't need God on this one. That's kind of sad, right? We don't pick such moments; we only have the choice to respond to them. Allow yourself the assumption that God wants to talk to you and be open to listening to what is placed in your mind and in your heart. Be mindful that anything from God is consistent with His word and it's helpful to discuss these insights with a pastor of church leader.

Review

Our lives are turned upside down by the loss of a loved one. Our minds are in a fog most of the time and even our day-to-day activities can be confusing. We don't want to get stuck here. We need a plan, a map to help us get going in the right direction. We know that after the numbness wears off, we must deal with the disorganization caused by our loss. Once we get a handle on things, we must reorganize things in an effective manner for ourselves. William Worden gives us the four tasks of grief: acknowledge the loss, express the emotions of grief, adapt, and restructure the painful thoughts into pleasant memories. The Church Softball Story provides an analogy that compares key elements of the game to display useful tools we can use in our recovery effort: take inventory, recognize weaknesses, seek help, follow a plan, integrate encouraging people into your life and listen to God's voice.

Things to Know

*Always review and implement the previously suggested, "Things to Know" and "Things to Do" from the earlier chapters. Continue to add to your story. Keep writing, making notes and dating them.

1. *Time Does Not Heal All Wounds.* Time is a useful tool to help us process grief, but it does not end all suffering. Grief is a lifelong process that can ebb and flow over time. The initial hurt and shock of grief will subside but the missing and yearning will stay with most.
2. *Defer Major Decisions.* Many people are tempted to sell the house, enter a new relationship, or make other major financial and relational decisions before they're ready. Even if the death of your loved one was anticipated due to a long-term illness, it takes time to unwind and separate from one person before being joined with another.
3. *Seek the Assistance of a Financial Expert.* The death of a loved one may trigger several financial situations one has to prepare for. Seek the advice of an expert who can unravel the benefits and remaining obligations resulting from your situation. They will be able to unlock the obscurities of your polices and advise on tax matters.

Things to Do

1. *Create New Routines.* Now is the time to do things you never previously had time for. Join clubs, take lessons, create, learn new things, travel, or volunteer. Volunteering is a great way to divert attention from yourself while meeting the needs of others.
2. *Find Ways to Honor You Loved One.* Donate to a charity in the name of your loved one, start a scholarship program in their name, do something as simple as plant a tree or organize an annual event.

3. *Allow Yourself to Move Forward.* One does not honor a loved one's memory through suffering and not progressing through grief. Your loved one would want you to be happy again, to discover a new life.

> **Frodo:** *Go back, Sam. I'm going to Mordor alone.*
> **Sam:** *Of course you are. And I'm coming with you.*

> —JRR Tolkien, Lord of the Rings

Chapter 6
Working Through The Pain Of Grief
Part 1: Self-Forgiveness

Wave Story

This is an excellent story copied from Reddit. I wish I knew who to give credit to but it's an anonymous source that has been shared on a few sites. It's one of the best perspectives of grief I have read. The story begins with someone who originated a post that simply stated, "My friend just died. I don't know what to do."

Several people responded but there's one old guy's comment that stood out from the rest:

"Alright, here goes. I'm old. What that means is that I've survived (so far) and a lot of people I've known and loved did not. I've lost friends, best friends, acquaintances, co-workers, grandparents, mom, relatives, teachers, mentors, students, neighbors, and a host of other folks. I have no children, and I can't imagine the pain it must be to lose a child. But here's my two cents.

I wish I could say you get used to people dying. I never did. I don't want to. It tears a hole through me whenever somebody I love dies, no matter the circumstances. But I don't want it to 'not matter.' I don't want it to be something that just passes. My scars are a testament to the love and the relationship I had for and with that person. And if the scar is deep, so was the love. So be it. Scars are a testament to life. Scars are a testament that I can love deeply and live deeply and be cut, or even gouged, and that I can heal and continue to live and continue to love. And the scar tissue is stronger than the original flesh ever was. Scars are a testament to life. Scars are only ugly to people who can't see.

As for grief, you'll find it comes in waves. When the ship is first wrecked, you're drowning, with wreckage all around you. Everything floating around you reminds you of the beauty and magnificence of the ship that was and is no more. And all you can do is float. You find some piece of the wreckage and you hang on for a while. Maybe it's some physical thing. Maybe it's a happy memory or a photograph. Maybe it's a person who is also floating. For a while, all you can do is float. Stay alive.

In the beginning, the waves are 100 feet tall and crash over you without mercy. They come 10 seconds apart and don't even give you time to catch your breath. All you can do is hang on and float. After a while, maybe weeks, maybe months, you'll find the waves are still 100 feet tall, but they come farther apart. When they come, they still crash all over you and wipe you out. But in between, you can breathe, you can function. You never know what's going to trigger the grief. It might be a song, a picture, a street intersection, the smell of a cup of coffee. It can be just about anything... and the wave comes crashing. But in between waves, there is life.

Somewhere down the line, and it's different for everybody, you'll find that the waves are only 80 feet tall. Or 50 feet tall. And while they still come, they come farther apart. You can see them coming. An anniversary, a birthday, or Christmas, or landing at O'Hare. You can see it coming, for the most part, and prepare yourself. And when it washes over you, you know that somehow you will, again, come out on the other side. Soaking wet, sputtering, still hanging on to some tiny piece of the wreckage, but you come out.

Take it from an old guy. The waves never stop coming, and somehow you don't really want them to. But you'll learn that you'll survive them. And other waves will come. And you'll survive them too. If you're lucky, you'll have lots of scars from lots of loves. And lots of shipwrecks."

Was our life better for having this love with us for the time we had them? Are we not better off by having experienced loving them than never knowing them at all? I love the wave story writer's perspective of grief in that he realizes that grief is the price of loving someone and that it's better to have loved and lost, than to never have loved. While we work through the pain of our loss, we can never allow ourselves to lose sight of the contributions our loved one made in our life. As we plod through the process of grief, we must always be mindful of what we had more than what we lost. Yes, it hurts to suffer a substantial loss like this, but we can never allow gratitude to slip too far from our conscious mind. Gratitude in grief? It sounds like an oxymoron but it's actually possible.

The Apostle Paul made bold statements such as his remarks in Phil. 1:21 *"For to me, to live is Christ and to die is gain."* How is it possible to possess this fearless attitude toward death? Paul continues to expound upon the topic of the power of resurrection in Phil 3:13-14, *"...forgetting what is behind and straining toward what is ahead, I press on toward the goal to win the prize for which God has called me heavenward in Christ Jesus."*

What is it that Paul is referring to when he states he is forgetting what is behind? Certainly, he's referring to his personal failures but beyond that, Paul was a prominent Pharisee and member of the Sanhedrin, trained by the highly regarded rabbi, Gamaliel, and a "Pharisee of Pharisees" as he described himself. As such, when he converted to Christianity, he was rejected by his own family, becoming an outcast. He was certainly married, had children, parents, position, respect, and wealth. Paul's conversion came at the cost of losing everything he loved and cherished in life. His method of dealing with such a significant and horrible loss was to put it out of his mind and focus on the prize. What is the prize? In I Thes 4:13-14, the key for processing grief for those of faith is stated,

*"Brothers and sisters, we do not want you to be uninformed about those who sleep in death, so that **you do not grieve like the rest of mankind, who have no hope**. For we believe that Jesus died and rose again, and so we believe that God will bring with Jesus those who have fallen asleep in him."*

Those of us with faith do not grieve like those outside the church because we have hope. This hope that we have is not to be misconstrued as a "Hail Mary" pass to the endzone on the final play of the game, but our hope in the resurrected Christ. The death, burial and resurrection of Christ is not simply a fantastical tale contained within the church, but a historical fact witnessed by thousands of people and documented in the both the writings of eyewitnesses and secular historians. I enjoy listening to the sermons of Andy Stanley, Lead Pastor of Buckhead Church in the Atlanta area. He often refers to Jesus's brother, James, who became the pastor of the Church of Jerusalem. Stanley, interjecting humor in the statement: "What would it take for your own brother to acknowledge you were God? Your own brother!" History reveals that he and nearly all the original disciples died as martyrs, each proclaiming the resurrection of Christ until their final moments. As Stanley points out, people don't die for myths and stories. The singular event that changed the course of civilization wasn't the teaching of Jesus, it was the fact that he died, was buried, and rose from the dead. This is the blessed hope. This is why we don't grieve like those outside the church. I Cor 15:55 *"Where, O death, is your victory? Where, O death, is your sting?"*

The Uber Ride

At times I write fiction and need inspiration in the form of new faces and personalities to use as models for the characters I create. It's difficult to create these characters when my daily routine limits me to the same demographic each day. As an experiment to see more faces, I rode the San Diego trolley for several days and came across several interesting people. Although intriguing, I became frustrated with the experience due to the lack of exposure to individual personalities, as most passengers either rode in silence or their attention absorbed by their phones. My solution was to sign on for a month as a part-time Uber driver. The pay was dismal, so much so that I lost money in the process, but I met some great people and had wonderful conversations that I would have never been exposed to otherwise.

One busy weekend, I picked up a group from a club in San Diego's Gaslamp District. I could smell alcohol on them as soon as the trio entered the car but that was common with fares generated from this part of town. After engaging them in conversation I discovered that the young ladies were relatively new members of the U.S. Navy. As a veteran myself, their connection with the military served as a basis of a good conversation until the attention turned to me. I didn't want to deceive them, but I know how uneasy young enlisted people get around an officer so I evaded the question. Finally, I was asked directly what I did in the military, and I told them I was a Chaplain. From their perspective, if you're going to be trapped in a car with an officer, a Chaplain is not a bad first choice because they aren't so scary—unless you've been out drinking and creating mischief which makes it a little worse. When the word, "Chaplain" came out of my mouth, the car went notably silent until one of the three spoke up and said, "We're all going to Hell now!"

After our laughter subsided, I discovered this group was comprised of church kids. They were now riddled with self-imposed guilt and before I could assure them there was no judgment on my part, one of the women, perhaps looking for an escape clause, thought to challenge my claim of being a Chaplain and asked me what my favorite bible verse and sermon was. I told her, *Psalm 103:10-12, "He does not treat us as our sins deserve or repay us according to our iniquities. For as high as the heavens are above the earth, so great is his love for those who fear him; as far as the east is from the west, so far has he removed our transgressions from us."* They wanted to hear more so I was given the opportunity to provide a sermonette to them until we arrived at our destination a few minutes later. When I looked up, the three were wiping tears and lingered in the car in a sort of stunned silence. One female sailor, with tears rolling down her cheeks, said Chaplain, "God can't forgive me for what I've done."

We locked eyes in the rearview mirror as I reverted to my past military persona, "Sailor, are you listening to me?"

"Yes sir, she said softly."

"I don't know what you've done in the past or will do in the future, but I know that God will forgive you."

We sat in silence for a moment, still locking eyes while tears rolled down her face until she uttered, "But…" She looked down and then stopped talking.

I waited for her to look back up and when she did, I asked her, "How many of your sins does God forgive?"

A slight smiled appeared as she replied, "All of them."

The three exited my vehicle and huddled together as I drove away. I'm not sure what issues they were facing but I was grateful to have been part of what was obviously a divine appointment. I can only imagine across the country somewhere, there was a parent or two or three, praying that God would keep His hand on their babies and keep them safe. On this side, there were three church kids sowing some wild oats who came to realize that God loved them enough to send them a Chaplain in the middle of the night.

One of the initial steps we can take in working through the pain of grief is to relieve ourselves of guilt. Guilt is the poisonous bite that if left untreated, will travel through our veins, and capture our heart. We can't allow guilt to establish root in our lives as it will steer us off course and delay our best efforts to recover. Yes, it's true, we may have done something different, or better, or at a different time. And even if an event was entirely due to our negligence, ignorance, or lack of effort, it doesn't change the final outcome, nor does it change God's grace. We are forgiven.

Sometimes we reflect upon our last words or our last contact with an individual and it may have lacked the loving contact we now wish we would have had. Our final communication may have been altogether unpleasant. There are a hundred different ways we can beat ourselves up over our mistakes or perceived mistakes. Whether real or imagined, guilt can weigh us down in the bereavement process. The passage in Psalm 103:3b is clear in that we serve a God *"who forgives all your sins"* and in Psalm 103:11-12, removes them *"as far as the east is from the west"* because His love for us is as *"high as the heavens are above the earth."*

Why do we have such a difficult time accepting God's forgiveness? It often stems from our perception of God the Father. Many of us have had childhood experiences that resulted in a combination of issues dealing with trust and authority figures. Being a victim of childhood abuse myself, I know it impacts heavily on my perception of God as a loving father. Even in a home absent of abuse, having very imperfect earthly fathers as a model can effectively distort our perception of God the Father.

Dodger Stadium Usher Story

During my first couple of years of college, I had a great part-time job working as an usher for the Los Angeles Dodgers. As a young man, I was amazed that I was actually paid to watch the Dodgers play baseball. Of course, there was more to the job than simply donning the Dodger blue sport coat and placing a straw hat on my head. Between innings we stood in a visible location and directed people to the nearest restrooms, phone booths (pre-cellphone days), concessions and on rare occasions, handled a matter with lost and found.

While working a busy afternoon game during the playoffs, I was assigned to a section in the upper decks and stood in position on one side of the tunnel as a throng of fans rushed past me. Situated across the tunnel from me was a young Asian girl, perhaps five years-old, who was obviously out of place as she timidly stood with her back glued to the wall. At times I could barely see her through the forest of legs that streamed between us. I made my way over to her, bent down to her level and asked if she was lost. Tears flowed down her cheeks as she nodded yes. I offered her my hand and she immediately responded by placing her tiny hand in mine. Since it was a playoff game, hundreds of people were rushing past us like a swarm of bees. I kept her close to me as I scanned the crowd, searching for a frantic looking parent, but did not immediately locate anyone. Having wrestled our way through half the crowd, I finally noticed an Asian man standing next to a tubular-steel railing with a worrisome expression. The place he occupied was situated forty feet above the level below. With the child in tow, we finally came to a break in the crowd where daddy and daughter's eyes met, and she ran into his arms. Once in his arms, the father lifted her up, and then tossed her over the railing and into the seats forty feet below.

My apologies dear reader. That is NOT how the story ends. I

know I risked making you upset with me, but the part about the father throwing his lost daughter over the railing is not true. The story is true but that's not how it ended. Why? I obviously want to make a point. God does not throw us over the railing when we get lost, when we mess up, when we fail, make mistakes, or even turn our backs on Him.

Grief recovery, for the Christian, begins and ends with love. It begins with the love we have for another and ends as we understand the depth of God's love for humanity and the eternity that awaits thereafter. After stockpiling over six hundred laws in the Old Testament, Jesus reduced the laws of God to two—to love God with all your heart, soul and mind, and to love others as we love ourselves. On the eve of His arrest and crucifixion, Jesus reduced it to the single command to love others as I have loved you. Jesus offered Himself as a sacrifice for us. That's love. Don't let your familiarity with this verse ruin its impact but contemplate the love invested by God for each of us in the passage (Jn. 3:16), "For God so loved the world that whosoever believes in Him should not perish but have everlasting life." Love requires the ability to choose and when humanity chose disobedience, there was a price to pay. Jesus stepped forward and accepted the cruel and sacrificial death on a Roman cross as the means to repair the damage done by our disobedience. What is required of us? Only to trust. God so loved He gave. We love Him back by trusting what He says is true. If what God says is true, He has removed the power of death and we no longer need to fear the grave. We trust in God's forgiveness and we in turn, accept forgiveness for ourselves and forgive others.

As for the rest of the story at Dodger Stadium, allow me to convey the real ending and motive behind the story. As stated, we were in the middle of a throng of hundreds of people who were rushing about trying to get settled before the playoff game started. Then something magical happened. Although I could see the young girl's father, he could not see his daughter by my side, nor could she see him through the crowd. But as I stood sandwiched in the crowd, one person at a time realized the dynamic of what was happening and stopped to make a gap. Some held out their arms as a makeshift barrier to hold the crowd at bay and for a moment, people stopped buying hot dogs, sodas, and souvenirs so as to witness this event. A hush came over the small section of Dodger Stadium as this chain reaction resulted in a pathway formed between father and daughter. The father wasn't aware of what was happening until the final second when his daughter saw him and popped out between legs and rushed into his arms. The crowd was so drawn into the father-daughter reunion that scores of people responded with a collective, "Awww…" After a brief pause, the area returned to the same chaotic environment that it was only seconds before.

What is the point of the story and why the deceptive ending? I wanted to illustrate that when we, as God's children, become lost or stray from where we're supposed to be, God doesn't abandon us. As ludicrous as the thought of a father tossing his daughter over the railing is, how much more so would it be for God, the Perfect Father, to do anything similar to us? I'm not sure why the father and daughter were separated. Perhaps he told her to wait for him by the railing, but she became frightened standing next to the steep drop and moved but was inadvertently swept away by the crowd and finally came to a place she never intended to be. Losing someone we love sometimes moves us to a place in life with which we are unfamiliar. In our grief, it's easy to become displaced, disoriented and leave the safety of what we know and end up stuck with our backs to the wall as a sea of legs pass before us. Fortunately, God doesn't send an adolescent kid dressed in Dodger blue to your rescue. Instead, it's the Holy Spirit, the Comforter who stands alongside of us, reassures us of God's love and provides us with renewed hope and confidence in our faith. God's welcoming hand is extended and all we have to do is trust Him enough to reach up and take it.

Review

Three stories were utilized in this chapter. First, the unknown writer of the "Wave Story" described how grief hits us like large waves that dissipate in size and intensity over time. Life happens between the waves. The "Uber Story" was about three church kids who were new U.S. Navy recruits, perhaps on their first leave, out partying and violating their deeply held moral values. The lesson learned is that God forgives our sins—all of them. The problem that remains is that even after repentance, we sometimes feel guilty for things forgiven. One of the obstacles we face in grief recovery is guilt. Nothing we do after a loved one passes is going to change the past. Most often the things we feel guilty for are things for which we neither had the power nor choice to control. For those mistakes we were responsible for, God forgives. The reason we have such difficulty in accepting forgiveness is often due to the imperfect image of a father we experienced in childhood. The third story, "The Dodger Stadium Usher Story" illustrates the true love of the Father versus our sometimes distorted image of a father's love.

In the first three chapters we examined our view of God, eternity, and mapped out our journey of grief. In the three chapters that followed we examined the importance of the funeral service and prioritizing precious memories. This was followed by a story that outlined a plan to establish a direction in our journey of grief. Finally, the most recent stories display how guilt and the acceptance of God's forgiveness impacts our journey of grief.

In the upcoming few chapters, we are going to continue to examine how to work through the pain of grief by forgiving others, then we will look at the obstacles we face and how to deal with "triggers" or things that suck us back into acute or the fresh painfulness of grief. The final few chapters will explore methods and models that will lay the foundation for a positive outlook for our days to come.

Things to Know

*Always review and implement the previously suggested, "Things to Know" and "Things to Do" from the earlier chapters. Continue to add to your story. Keep writing, making notes and dating them.

1. "Triggers" are circumstances and events that pull us back into a state of intense emotion and grief. They are

part of everyone's grief experience. One can be triggered by seeing someone who looks like our departed love, a familiar smell, the sight of children playing, a couple holding hands, an expression, location, song, or an annual event such as holidays, a birthday or anniversary.

2. There are several different types of grief. Sudden grief happens unexpectedly whereas prolonged grief is the result of a long-term injury or illness. Complicated or prolonged grief is when someone is unable to accept the reality of their loss and move past the initial pain of intense grief. As a result, their condition does not improve. Disenfranchised grief is a form of bereavement that incurs when a loss cannot be openly acknowledged, socially sanctioned or publicly mourned.

3. Secondary losses are the ancillary losses we experience in addition to our loved one. We may lose financial security, relationships, access, some opportunities and dreams, to name a few.

Things to Do

1. Continue writing, journaling, and recording your journey through grief. You do not have to be a great writer—chicken scratches and bullet points will work— the goal is to record your story and monitor your progress. The *Comfort in Grief Workbook* may serve as an aid in this process. In the end, you will be able to tell your story to someone else, e.g., *"I was completely broken here, but here I started to see a glimmer of hope. I fell back into a lonely state here, was triggered by a holiday here but made it through that and now I'm here. I don't feel the intense pain nearly as often and I'm confident I will make it back to some sense of normalcy but I'm still working on it. As I look back over this past year, I never thought I'd be here. I can see the improvement. I'm still sad at times but I'm going to be okay."*

2. What holiday or anniversary is approaching? Plan an activity with a friend or family member. Keep yourself from being isolated or alone on such days.

3. Set aside time to grieve. Many of us must return to work. Inform co-workers that you're grieving the loss of a loved one and at times you may not be yourself but you're improving. Let them know what you need from them. When you're home, review old photos, videos, and messages—allow yourself to feel the emotions of grief.

Guilt is the poisonous bite that if left untreated, will travel through our veins and capture our heart.

Chapter 7
Working Through The Pain Of Grief
Part 2: Forgiving Others

The hurts and wounds we incur from those who were supposed to nurture and protect us have a profound and lasting impact on our lives. I only write the following lines after prayerful contemplation. I am willing to expose this unspoken and shameful side of my life as a means to facilitate healing and solutions for others who have experienced similar issues.

Surviving Abusive Relationships

My mom was the youngest child of eleven children who grew up on a farm in Arkansas. At the age of thirteen, she was desperate to leave home and do something different—anything to get her away from the hard work of farm life and the brutality of her father. She was physically mature for her age—tall, busty, and beautiful… immediately capturing the attention of my nineteen-year-old father. After a very brief courtship, he convinced her to cross the state line, lie about her age and marry him. I was born when mom was fifteen, my brother when she was seventeen and by the age of nineteen we had relocated to San Diego where dad was serving in the military.

Dad was a brutal alcoholic who lived to drink. After the military, he worked as a custodian or maintenance worker for large corporations. It was an environment that allowed him to stagger into work and sleep in a closet for a couple of hours to recover from the night before. Our homelife was a nightmare. By the age of twelve we were left at home alone several nights each week while mom and dad went out drinking. We were actually okay being alone, since it was a time we felt safe. Dad was the jealous type so if a man displayed any attention toward my mother, he'd beat her when they got home. It became a common routine—yelling, screaming, slaps, punches... it wasn't safe to go to sleep until we heard dad snoring, and that was usually after two in the morning. Domestic violence laws had not yet been implemented, and there was little the police could do unless a spouse was willing to sign an official complaint. Mom was young and naïve, and no matter how many times he beat her, she never signed a complaint and always took him back.

One night as dad had mom pinned against the wall, I dared to peek around the corner to see what he was doing to her. He delivered two hard punches to her abdomen, the second one doubling her over. As her head came down and the air escaped her lungs, his uppercut landed on her jaw. I can still remember the clacking sound it made as her teeth were smashed together. I was only twelve and obviously no match for dad, but I couldn't stand there and watch him beat her like that. Dressed in only my underwear briefs, I jumped on his back and attempted to pull him off of her. He quickly turned, sending me skidding across the linoleum floor until I collided with a cabinet. As I stood to my feet, he staggered over to me and thew a devastating round house punch toward my head. I had the good sense to duck and his fist smashed a bowl behind me. I thought I was going to die but before he wound up to deliver another punch, my ten-year-old brother copied my earlier effort and climbed on dad's back, and with the same result.

The odd dynamic was that my brother was his favorite son. He was compliant and easily controlled and I was the opposite. Regardless, dad staggered toward him on the other side of the room while mom attempted to shield him. Unable to land a direct punch, dad began kicking my brother in the face. When I saw both mom and little brother covered in blood, I knew my turn was next. My outcome was likely to be much worse, so I ran. I darted out the back door while dad continued to focus his wrath on mom and my brother. The back door was easy enough to exit but there was a split bamboo gate that trapped me in the back yard. My hands were shaking so hard, I lost dexterity in my fingers and couldn't unlatch the wiring that held the gate together. The gate was a couple of feet higher than my twelve-year-old frame and I couldn't jump over it, so I finally decided to lean against the top of it until my weight caused me to spill over to the opposite side. That decision saved my life.

By the time dad staggered out the back door, I had already run across the main road, up the hill and stood hiding in an avocado orchard. If any good came out of me running, it was that dad had left mom and brother alone so he could find me. He searched an empty field near the house for nearly an hour with a flashlight and club in hand, "Come on out Eddy. I'm not going to hurt you."

I found an old, abandoned truck in the orchard, wiped off the spider webs and slept inside for a couple of hours before the sun came up. When I saw that my dad had left for work, I ran home. Unfortunately, all the kids from school were lined up at the bus stop and I had to run by them, clothed in only my underwear.

I wish I could say that this was the worst of it, but it wasn't. This event simply led to the first and only confrontation with mom on the issue. Dad left the house when he sobered up and realized what he had done. Mom wanted to allow him to return to the house, but both my brother and I said firmly, "If you take him back, he's going to do it again, and again. We're not big enough to protect you and we'll never try to help again because he will kill us." She took him back anyway.

It was in this environment that God prepared a new way of life for me. My first exposure to church people was in the sixth grade when I was twelve years old. One of my classmates and friends was a kid named Danny. He was probably the only kid in class who was as goofy looking as me, sporting thick glasses, and having ears that seemed to shoot straight out from each side of his head. I loved to make him laugh or get him excited because when he blushed, his ears turned red too. As it turned out, Danny's church had an upcoming roller skating event and he invited me to attend. Church people were really an odd sort when I first met them. They verbalized loving one another, displayed affection, and seemed to laugh and smile a lot. Being around these people was like being in a foreign country and so different from the reality I knew. The people were odd to me, but in a good kind of way. When Danny invited me to go to church with him the following day, I accepted.

This wasn't my first time in church. My first church experience was when I was about eight years old. Our Lady of Perpetual Help, a Catholic church down the hill from our house, was a building that my brother and I had yet to explore. The doors were open, so we walked into the empty building and were immediately awed by the stained glass and high ceilings. We stood, wide-eyed and curious. There was some type of container filled with fluid next to the door. We touched it, and then drank some. It tasted like water, but we couldn't figure out why it was next to the door and why they didn't put a drinking fountain there so everyone could have a drink. We cautiously walked down the aisle as our only point of reference was *The Wizard of Oz*. If he was real, he probably lived here. There were candles too, and some were lit. For two young boys, it was like an invitation to light some too. We weren't there very long, probably just long enough to get God's attention and leave before we were struck by lightning.

We lived in a small, rural community, so everyone knew everyone and by the time we got home, my parents already knew that we had gone inside the church. We were just curious—we didn't break anything. Okay, we drank a little holy water, but we didn't know what it was and I think maybe God may have been slightly amused by our irreverence. Dad decided to act on it at the dinner table. Even completely sober he was yelling something about, "No kid of his was going to cause him embarrassment..." I don't remember the entirety of his speech as he came up behind me and hit me in the back of the head with such force, my face hit the dinner plate, shattering it into several pieces. My face was cut and bloodied, resulting in a scar I wore for forty years. I wasn't overly eager to go back to church, but God had other plans as I was now twelve and giving church a second try.

I remember being in Sunday School with about fifteen other kids in our age group. Mrs. Houlihan was our teacher and the lesson for this particular Sunday was about some character named Moses. Moses? I was always a pretty good student, but I had never heard of Moses. As the lesson began, everyone else was nodding and smiling. The entire class seemed to know who Moses was—even Danny, and I was way smarter than Danny. Ten minutes into the lesson, I couldn't stand it anymore and my hand shot up, "Mrs. Houlihan, who is Moses?" The class laughed at me, but I didn't care. Mrs. Houlihan was a really nice lady who appeased me with a quick explanation and moved on with her lesson.

Two weeks later I went back to church and this week's lesson was on Jesus. As Mrs. Houlihan began talking about Jesus, I looked around the room and as before, everyone was nodding and smiling as though they all knew about Jesus—even Danny. Ten minutes into the lesson, I couldn't stand it any longer and I shot up my hand, blurting out the question, "Mrs. Houlihan, who's Jesus?" Everyone laughed at me again, but Mrs. Houlihan looked me straight in the eyes and when she realized my question was sincere, she turned her back to the class and silently wept. Danny slugged me in the arm for making Mrs. Houlihan cry. After she gathered herself, Mrs. Houlihan gave me a quick explanation about Jesus and after class she hugged me, told me she loved me and that she would be praying for me. I wasn't sure what praying was, but it was nice to feel loved. I suspect I became Mrs. Houlihan's pet project after that, and she was determined to love me into the Kingdom of God from that moment onward.

I continued to attend church with Danny for the weeks, months and years that followed. I didn't understand a lot about church, the stories that were told, or why they behaved the way they did. All I knew was that when I went to church, the people appeared to like having me there and, of course, there was Mrs. Houlihan. Everyone loved Mrs. Houlihan.

One night, not too long after beginning to attend the church, I sat in bed waiting in the early morning hour as mom and dad arrived home from the bar. Rather than lie down and pretend to be asleep as I usually did, I sat up and waited as the very predictable fighting began to rage in the next room. By now I had been exposed to another way of life and knew there was something oddly appealing about the crazy church people. As a twelve-year-old, I didn't understand much about God, but I saw God in the love that Mrs. Houlihan and the church people displayed toward me. This led to the first prayer of my life. "Jesus, if you're real like Mrs. Houlihan says you are, I need you." God heard my prayer and I felt something enter my body in waves that went around me, inside me and through me. It was a tingling sensation that seemed to have energy like wind, powerful in impact but gentle in touch. I had no idea what it was but at that moment, I knew in my twelve-year-old mind that God was real. I didn't understand anything on a theological basis, but God met me at a place where His reality became evident to me. I told Mrs. Houlihan what happened to me, and she instructed me to go forward when the pastor invited people to do so at the end of the service. I did what Mrs. Houlihan said and prayed the sinner's prayer as they told me to, but I knew in my heart that I met Jesus on my bed a few days earlier.

Fast forward a few years and our lives were filled with repeated abusive behavior—fights, beatings, and the destruction of property. Christmas and the holidays were always a nightmare as we usually spent them hiding out at a family friend's house. On more than one Christmas, my little brother and I watched our friend's kids open their presents while we received a charity gift of a pair of socks. The problem was not getting presents, it was getting them in one piece. When we returned home after Christmas, the tree and all the presents were found smashed to pieces. As an adult looking back, Christmas is not about materialism and "things" but in a child's mind and in a godless home, it was a time of glitter, lights, and gifts. The residual impact was returning to school and hearing what all your friends got for Christmas. Naturally, I avoided these conversations as I didn't want to explain that I received half of one thing and a smashed version of another.

At a time when most families lived off a single income, mom worked as a cocktail waitress and generated more income in tips than dad's meager wage as a maintenance man. Logic should have dictated that dad's life as a regular at the local drinking establishment was largely supported by her tips. On nights when she worked, he occupied his regular seat at the bar, smoking cheap cigars and chasing any woman who would pay attention to him.

We lived in a small house with a single bathroom so there was little privacy. In a disgusting, near nightly ritual, dad relentlessly begged mom for sex until she complied. Little brother and I were too young to know details, but we knew the squeaky bed would announce his successful plea and thirty seconds of magic. Once he staggered into my bedroom after being refused sex by mom. He cuddled up next to me, fondling my body and finally pressed himself against me in an attempt to sodomize me. At first, I thought he was so drunk he had mistaken me for mom. I screamed at him, "I'm not mom! I'm Eddy!" I looked back and he was laughing. I escaped being penetrated by sliding off the side of the mattress and sleeping through a cold and distressful night under the bed.

A few years passed and I witnessed the most brutal beating of my life. In one of his drunken rages, dad raped and beat mom in front of me. He beat her so severely there was blood coming from every orifice of her naked and unconscious body. As I trembled in fear and shock, he burned all the clothing she owned in the fireplace. Each time she regained consciousness, he beat her unconscious again until he tired of it and finally dragged her limp, naked body out into the street and left her there. I thought she was dead, but a passing motorist saw her and transported her to the hospital. To my astonishment, she survived. After she recovered in the hospital, she and my brother left… she finally left him. Mom wanted me to go with her, but I had a girlfriend, my first job and a car. I thought I could tolerate the situation by staying away from him, working a lot of hours, living my life, and staying in my room when he was there. It was a good idea in theory, but it didn't last long.

Dad kicked me out of the house at the age of seventeen, near the beginning of my senior year of high school. My enraged and overly intoxicated father threw everything I owned out in the street, making it clear in his rant that he wasn't going to have a "long-haired queer" living in his house. My hair wasn't long, and my heterosexual orientation was never an issue. I had a job and had been working since the age of sixteen. I paid for my own car, gas, insurance, clothing and ate many of my meals at the fast-food restaurant where I worked. Looking back from the vantage point of time and experience, I can see that the real issue was dad's inability to accept responsibility for his own failures and self-imposed misery. Generally speaking, those who aren't self-aware or who lack the fortitude to examine their own lives, commonly victimize others while claiming to be the victim themselves. In my situation, I had nowhere else to go so I secretly lived in my car for several weeks. By arriving to school early in the morning and pretending to work out in the gym, I was able to use the shower and maintain the appearance of a normal life. Soon thereafter, a friend's family heard of my situation and took me in, allowing me to finish high school while living with them on a dairy farm. Sadly, it was about the same time mom and my brother decided to return home.

Approximately six months later I was driving to my adopted family's home from a late-night date. As my car rounded a bend on a rural two-lane road, my attention was drawn to a cluster of flashing emergency lights that had gathered around an upside-down vehicle. The car's roof had been crushed nearly to the level of the tops of the doors, and it was obvious to anyone seeing the automobile that serious injuries or death resulted from the tragic accident. I was too curious not to look but after quickly scanning the scene and seeing nothing, I decided to drive on. I'm not sure what made me glance back one last time. My eyes fixated on the upside-down license plate and within a moment, the image became clear to me in its proper orientation—RDN 110. I remember the license plate number to this day. It was my parents' car!

I did an immediate U-turn and stopped my car within a few feet of the crushed vehicle. Mom was a thirty-two-year-old cocktail waitress, and I immediately knew she was in the car because the entire area was glittered with the coins of her tips. By the time I exited my vehicle, a Deputy Sheriff approached me with a stern look that quickly dissipated when he noted my demeanor. My knees were wobbly, and I was obviously distressed. My conversation with him was a scatter of noise as my attention was captivated by the gurney being loaded into the back of an ambulance.

I suspected the emergency responders would take the freeway route to the hospital while I, having grown up in this small country town, knew the shortcut over the hill. There was no ICU or Intensive Care Unit at that time, so I stood in the doorway to the emergency entrance as my parents were carted by me. Dad was the first. As usual, he reeked of alcohol, and it only took an instant to put all the pieces of the puzzle together in my mind. Dad was drunk, picked up mom from work and the two were headed home, probably arguing along the way. When dad drank, he perceived his driving skills to be on the level of a professional race car driver and in his mind, he was invincible. In childhood he often drove twice the speed limit and delighted in the fact that he could scare us to tears. When I got older, if I smelled alcohol on him, I always elected to walk for miles rather than get in the car with him. Mom didn't have that choice. Her work was fifteen miles from home and the cocktail lounge didn't close until the early morning hours. Dad often expressed his alcohol induced rage while driving to intimidate and terrify her into submission.

When mom was wheeled by, she initially looked unscathed in that there was no evidence of serious cuts or lacerations, but she did have a big lump in the back of her neck. I stood in the doorway to the room where she was placed face-down on a gurney. I'm not sure how she knew I was in the room, or how she was still conscious, but she began to scream at me, "Get out! Eddy, get out of here!"

I stood my ground. The nurse looked in my direction with a sorrowful expression, but it became obvious that she wasn't going to force me to leave. I later learned that mom's neck had been broken between the second and third vertebrae and everyone thought she had only minutes of life remaining. The compassionate nurse didn't want to rob me of my final moments with my mother. When it became apparent to mom that I wasn't leaving, her tone changed and in a soft voice she asked, "How do I look?"

I had been with my mother since they brought her into the hospital, so no one had time to inform her of the situation. I was only seventeen and possessed a very superficial medical knowledge, but I told her, "Mom, you have a big lump in your neck. I think your neck is broken."

Mom didn't respond and we stood there in silence for a minute until a burly physician came in the room, grabbed me by both shoulders and guided me into the hallway. Once out of earshot of others, he turned to face me and with his hands still on my shoulders, "Son, I don't know how else to say this to you, but your mom is going to die."

I knew the situation was serious but on TV and in the movies, the doctors always provided patients with their odds of survival. I wanted to negotiate a deal with the big, burly physician so that my mom had a chance to live. The physician didn't appear to want to make a deal with me and he continued to insist that she would be dead within a few hours. I patiently asked one last time, "What if she lives twenty-four hours? What are her chances then?"

The physician seemed a little perturbed by my persistence, but he finally buckled, "If she lives twenty-four hours, I'll give her a 10% chance of living."

The large man released his grasp on me, thinking the conversation was over but I grabbed his hand before it left my shoulder. Ten percent wasn't enough and in an act of boldness I blurted out, "What about forty-eight hours? What percentage will you give me for forty-eight hours?"

He stared at me in silence for a couple of seconds and then finally conceded, "I'll give her a fifty-fifty chance if she survives forty-eight hours!" He abruptly pulled away from me and left me standing alone in the hallway. Regardless of his blunt bedside manner, I now had something I could work with and odds I could handle. The big, lingering question at hand was, what can I do to keep mom alive for forty-eight hours?

It was close to three o'clock in the morning when I called my pastor, waking him up from a dead sleep. "Pastor Runyan, this is Eddy Keebler. I'm so sorry I woke you up this early but, my mom needs forty-eight hours..." He joyfully received my information and passed the phone to his wife who ran the prayer chain for the church. She assured me that scores of people would be praying through the night for my mom and for me not to worry. My parents had never attended a single service at their church so I was amazed they would do this for me. I was the only Christian in my family and was still very young in my faith. Church people still appeared kind of odd to me at this time in life. I couldn't resist the mental image of visualizing all these wonderfully crazy Christian people getting out of bed all over town in the middle of the night to pray for my mom. I felt a little guilty for asking that of them, but I was desperate, and I only needed forty-eight hours.

I left the hospital shortly after talking to Pastor Runyan and returned the following morning. I was nervous walking up to the nurse's station but calmly asked, "Is my mom still alive?" I suppose I should have told them my name, but they seemed to know who I was. A nurse looked up and smiled at me, then circling around the counter, took me by the arm and said she would take me to see her. As we entered the room my eyes scanned the area for her familiar long dark hair, but I didn't see her. The nurse stopped at the end of one of the beds but the only thing near me was someone with a shaved head in a circular device shaped like a human-sized hamster wheel. I thought the person was a man with two horrible spikes protruding from his head as he lie facing the ground. I attempted to keep walking forward to find my mom and was beginning to get agitated with the nurse for not letting me go. I explained to her as politely as possible that I wanted to see my mom and in a sweet voice she said, "Honey, this is your mom." I looked on the floor and noticed a mirror reflecting her familiar face. I tried not to look over-whelmed, but I was. My beautiful mom was strapped into a circular bed with metal spikes coming out of her head. It was difficult to absorb the sight, but God answered our prayers, and she was alive.

Even after surviving the first twenty-four hours, the hospital staff put off setting the remaining half dozen broken bones in mom's body. No one in San Diego medical history had survived such a severe break and lived through the ordeal up to this time, so the medical staff didn't expect a different result with mom. I suppose they weren't taking into consideration that I had a couple hundred crazy Christian people awake at all hours of the day praying for her. Mom lived forty-eight hours, and then a week, and then two. After about a month they decided to set her other broken bones and two weeks later they shipped her off to a rehabilitation hospital.

Mom was understandably angry and bitter after the accident. She knew that if she were fortunate enough to live at all, the only life she had to look forward to was one in a hospital bed and dependent on twenty-four hour care. To add to her misery, church people started popping up everywhere. If Pastor Runyan wasn't there, it appeared that every shift of nurses had a Christian assigned to mom. Mom used to complain, "If this hospital had a hundred nurses and only one was a Christian, I'd get that one." Of course, she knew I was a Christian so she tolerated all of us, even though she thought we were all "nuts" as she would say. In the months that followed during her rehab, I spent so much time at the hospital I learned how to do wheelies in mom's wheelchair, and frequently raced the young paraplegics down the hallway. They always won.

About a year after being in rehab, mom agreed to pray with one of her Christian nurses and she became a Christian "nut" herself. Most quadriplegics of that day only lived a year or two. Even those who were young and in great condition typically didn't survive more than ten years. We prayed that God would give her forty-eight hours and God gave mom another thirty-four years. During this time, as part of her therapy, she learned to paint with oil using a brush that she held in her mouth. In time she became a popular local artist and gave her testimony in several churches while displaying her artwork.

Dad's journey was completely different. He said he became a Christian when he regained consciousness in the hospital but upon his release, he brought a nurse to the house. She introduced herself as "my new momma" and dad had sex with her in the adjoining bedroom while I was still there. Mom's life was hanging in balance as dad continued to drink, chase women, and seemed entirely unaffected by mom's condition. I am aware that Christians aren't perfect and growing in faith involves a lot of missteps and failures on the pathway to maturity. It's a growing experience and a life of repeated failure and forgiveness but I can say with assurance that I was disappointed by the fruit of dad's life.

In the years that followed, mom became increasingly attached to her faith while dad continued to sow seeds of deception. Rather than accept responsibility for what he had done, he began to tell everyone that it was mom who was driving the car and despite what she had done, he was there by her side, taking care of her. In time, dad figured out that he made more money from the state by staying home and taking care of mom rather than working fulltime as a janitor. He had reclaimed his cash cow via mom's disability and was receiving the accolades of all by portraying himself as the hero of the story.

Later he volunteered for a "food ministry" whose purpose was intended to feed the homeless and those in need. He used the higher valued meat items as a sort of currency with area merchants in exchange for car repairs and other goods and services. When I asked him about this, he stated with authority, "The homeless don't have refrigerators, they can't use this." He had no comment on the needy as he saw himself as the neediest. In typical fashion, he picked out very visible locations within the community and worked a couple of hours passing out bottled water and crackers to the homeless. He either consumed, traded, or gifted to friends what remained. Perhaps one of the reasons he held me in such disdain was that I saw through the venire of his manufactured image and never gave him the adoration he always sought from others.

I attempted to reestablish a relationship with him later in life, but he never displayed evidence of a moral compass. In his old age, his driving skills diminished, and he was involved in a couple of fender benders. One more accident and he could lose his driving privileges. One foggy morning he sideswiped another vehicle in a hit and run. He reported to the police that I was driving his truck at the time, and it wasn't until a year later I called to see why my insurance premiums had increased. It was due to this accident that was now on my record. On another occasion I owned a used SUV and was preparing to register it with the DMV when he offered to do it for me. I was gullible enough to let him. He registered the vehicle in his own name and after a spat with him, he took possession of it.

Mom died at the age of sixty-six. The forty-eight hours we prayed for turned into thirty-four years. Her death certificate states she died of complications of quadriplegia, but it doesn't include the circumstances of her death. It doesn't mention that fires raged through San Diego that year and residents were told to evacuate. I know it's a major undertaking to lift mom into her wheelchair, get her situated in the donated van equipped with a lift, and drive to a hotel to repeat the process all over in reverse. Yes, I know it's a lot of effort. But by staying she was forced to inhale the smoke generated by the fires. Her compromised lungs could not cough up enough of the flam and she suffocated to death. Dad often bragged, "We were married 53 years. She's the only woman I ever loved." His proclamation reeked of self-righteousness, as though he had a long, happy, and devoted relationship.

I was living in Colorado at the time, and I remember getting a call from my brother, letting me know that mom had died. He said he had seen her at times with bruises on her face. Mom always made excuses for dad but it's apparent that he never stopped beating her. The thought of never being able to talk to mom again made my heart sad but, if I'm being entirely candid, I was largely relieved. Her tortured life was over.

Where do we begin to forgive someone who has violated us at such a core level of our being and over such an extended period of time? It may be difficult to process, but forgiveness has little to do with the person who abused us. Forgiveness begins and ends with us. The abuser has little input in the process and no control over it. We simply choose to manage the state of our heart and mind by taking away their power. Forgiveness allows for that. I know that is contrary to all we think to be true. If there was a magic button we could push resulting in the abusers being chained and punished for what they did, most of us would push it. The sad reality is punishing the abuser offers little relief as revenge doesn't remove the stain of the offense. Only forgiveness does that. Revenge doesn't satisfy the injustice of the event, doesn't remove the memory—it doesn't put a period at the end of the sentence or allow us to sleep peacefully at night—only forgiveness does that.

In relation to our grief journey, there are certain emotional obstacles that hinder and can even block our progress through grief recovery. Among them are guilt, anger and unforgiveness. These unresolved issues have the capacity to divert our journey of grief into what is often referred to as complicated or prolonged grief. Simply stated, we can get bogged down or stuck in our progress if we don't find a way to fix it. But how do we do that?

In a paraphrase of the Gospel of Matthew (Mt 18:21-22) Peter asks Jesus, how many times should we forgive someone who sins against us and suggests seven as a solution. Jesus replies, "Seventy times seven" or, in other words, an unlimited number of times. Unlimited forgiveness? Doesn't that make us everyone's punching bag? The simple answer is "no."

To put the matter in context, the two greatest commandments are mentioned as loving God with all your heart, soul, and mind and the second is to love others as we love ourselves. In reading this Passage (Mt. 22:37-40) our minds tend to absorb loving God as our highest priority—we all get that. But in reading the second commandment of the two, it's easy to focus on the "loving others" component without pausing to think about, "loving ourselves." How can we effectively love others unless we realize the depth of love God has for us and in turn become aware of our own unique value? If we are not aware of our value and cannot love ourselves, how are we able to demonstrate God's love to others?

What does this mean? Self-love and self-respect are repeatedly demonstrated by Jesus in His interactions with the toxic religionist of the first century. Jesus would not allow himself to be a punching bag and did not tolerate abuse. He frequently called out the Pharisee's double standards, evil intentions and confronted them by identifying them with names, i.e., sons of snakes (snakes were symbols of Satan or demons) and whited sepulchers (hypocrites). In another passage He drove the moneychangers and con artists out of the temple (Mk 11:15-17). Self-love demands truth. Self-love will not tolerate allowing ourselves to be abused by individuals and institutions who seek to gaslight us into believing their abuse is justified. Love for such people and institutions ends at an arm's length as we have a right to preserve our health and sanity. We must value our own lives enough to stand up for ourselves and to preserve and protect the unique qualities God gave to each of us.

But what about Jesus dying on the cross? Didn't He ultimately submit to the abusers, and they defeated Him? No, the Pharisees attempted to kill Jesus several times and Jesus wouldn't allow it. Jesus never played by their rules and was always confrontational against their lies. The sacrifice of His life on Golgotha was known, planned, and completed as an act of His own will for the redemption of humanity. Jesus did not succumb to the will of His abusers; He simply demonstrated the depth of His love to humankind via the cross. When the abusers thought they had won... resurrection, checkmate.

Some may find this confusing, but my hope is that we understand that it's okay to love someone at an arm's length. Is this harsh? Unfortunately, a characteristic of those who exhibit personality disorders (discussed in more detail in the workbook) is their dysfunctional ability to reorganize and recreate a version of history that exists only in their minds. By the time these individuals have restructured and polished their recall of factual events, they have virtually erased all elements of their responsibility and wrongdoing from the narrative. Often, in the fray of the resulting conflict, they perceive themselves as the victim. Sadly, a deeper state of intimacy with such people will only be allowed if we acquiesce to their version of reality. If we oppose their view, we become the subject of relentless, demeaning, and malicious gaslighting as a means to shame us into compliance. Sometimes family members invest decades of their lives in an attempt to appease such personalities under the guise of religious duty and have only heartache as a reward.

As a hospice chaplain, I have encountered several situations with multiple siblings in the family, but of the group, one makes the decision to sacrifice a period of their life to care for the aging parent. We may be tempted to think that the adult child who made the sacrifice would be the most respected and valued by the ill parent, but the opposite is often true. The parent speaks fondly of the other children, their achievements, and their qualities, while being dismissive and unappreciative of the person making the sacrifice to stay. One individual gave up marriage, education, travel, and all she knew to serve her mother's needs for twenty years. At the end of her life, the mother treated the daughter who sacrificed her time and devotion with contempt, while welcoming her other children with an outward display of love and appreciation. The sacrificial daughter never understood that the dismissive and demeaning behavior was the result of her mother's personality disorder. The daughter was never good enough, so she stayed to earn that long awaited love and respect that never came.

Where do we draw the line to preserve our own lives and protect the ones we love and nurture?

The Apostle Paul (1 Cor. 5:11) was not shy in pointing out that we should not eat with "brothers" or those who claim to be followers of Jesus, who exhibit certain destructive behaviors. In other epistles he instructs believers with words such as, "avoid, remove, and do not associate." There is a reason for this. The church assembles with two specific purposes in mind—to glorify God and to build or encourage one another. If we maintain intimate relationships with those who willfully walk in disobedience, we not only repeatedly expose ourselves to their toxic behaviors but often come away from the encounter feeling unsettled in our spirit. This is not to say one should shun or act unloving to any degree. It's about learning to love at an arm's length, to offer support and encouragement without becoming absorbed by another's willful rebellion, lies, or denial. My closest friends are those with whom I can freely share my life events and faith. We openly discuss our journey of faith as well as the challenges, failures, and issues we are experiencing. I frequently come away from these encounters feeling heard, valued, understood, and encouraged.

The tightrope we walk with family members is in response to the question, how do we continue to honor father, mother, or sibling without subjecting ourselves to a lifetime of ongoing abuse? From the vantage point of grief recovery, we cannot begin to grieve until we acknowledge the problem and express our honest emotions as to how the situation impacts us. As such, for my own mental health, I cannot affirm dad's restructured story of his tranquil, long-term, and successful marriage to my mother. It may have been a wonderful marriage for him but for her, it was a living hell that she endured; an ongoing environment in which she was beaten, raped, cheated on and eventually one in which she sacrificed her health, mobility and finally her life. I witnessed and experienced the drunken cruelty myself so denial and acquiescing to a revamped reality does nothing to aid me in grief recovery. What then, is the solution? Forgiveness.

Forgiveness is the cure for smoldering anger and bitterness, each of which is toxic to our soul and spirituality. We forgive for our own self-healing, separated from the person and their acts against us. Beyond forgiveness, there is mercy. In the biblical story of Joseph, a young man sold into slavery by his own brothers, he was merciful toward his siblings when he was in the position of power. Mercy is that quality that compels us to bless those who have wronged us with our time, resources, and love when they are completely undeserving. Mercy is an act that demonstrates that forgiveness has taken root.

Review

Immediately following the loss of a loved one, we tend to do a deep dive into thoughts and emotions that may have been buried for years—or even decades. Situations and events that we convinced ourselves of being inconsequential were simply repressed. Now, with the cork released from the bottle, many such memories may surface. Tell the truth… we were abused. We must work though all the excuses and gaslighting, and call it out for what it was. Many of these people have moved on from our lives. Recall each one in your mind and allow yourself to remember what they did to you, and then forgive them. Release the negative power of that memory through forgiveness.

Love God with all your heart, soul, and mind; love others as you love yourself. Love yourself. God made us as a unique and special person, and we are unable to completely love others until we understand how lovely we are. God made us in His image. We cannot allow abusive people to strip us of His image in us or our self-image as God sees us. We can love toxic people at an arm's length. We are able to forgive people and are not obligated to incorporate them into our life or maintain intimacy with them. Forgive. The evidence of forgiveness is mercy.

Things to Know

*Always review and implement the previously suggested, "Things to Know" and "Things to Do" from the earlier chapters. Continue to add to your story. Keep writing, making notes and dating them.

1. Men have more personality disorders than women. Women read more than men. Most men will never read this.
2. Someone with a personality disorder repetitively engages in behaviors that others find offensive or problematic. Yet the individual does not understand why others think this way about their behavior, states Steven Hollon, PhD, a professor of psychology at Vanderbilt University. "They just don't see anything wrong with how they are acting."
3. There is good grief and bad grief. Good grief is when we process grief in a normal way and allow ourselves to go through the challenges of crying, lethargy, social withdrawal, questioning God, questioning personal choices, change of appetite, lack of sleep or sleeping too much, mental fog and a variety of emotions. Bad grief

prohibits us from normal function. We remain preoccupied by our loss in such a way that acute grief is prolonged, and we are not able to move on.

Things to Do

1. Make a list of the people in your life who have abused you. Look at their name, close your eyes, and allow yourself to see the event replay in your mind. If some memories are too scary, picture yourself in an empty room with Jesus. With His arm around you, enter the scene. If that too, is too much to contend with, avoid pictures and write down what you remember, in bullet points if necessary. When complete, either speak the words to the person in your mind, or write the words, "I forgive you."

2. Make a calendar and list all the upcoming holidays, anniversaries and special events once celebrated with our loved one. These days may be potentially devastating as they trigger the deep emotional bonds and reminders of our loss. Solicit family and friends to join you on these days for special activities.

3. Do something for someone in need. A simple donation is good, but a better idea is to utilize your personal time and energy to provide a meal, help clean a house, distribute food, work in a thrift shop or volunteer for a church or nonprofit organization.

"There is no love without forgiveness, and there is no forgive-ness without love."

— Bryant H. McGill

"Forgiveness is the fragrance that the violet sheds on the heel that has crushed it."

— Mark Twain

"To forgive is to set a prisoner free and discover that the pris-oner was you."

— Lewis B. Smedes

Chapter 8
Obstacles To Grief Recovery

Snakes Don't Scrape

I was a chubby little kid in the third grade. As fate would have it one of my best friends was a tall and trim kid named Sam, with the reputation of being the fastest runner in our grade. There was even a rumor circulating that he once beat a fifth grader. Hanging out with Sam during recess was awkward because I dreaded hearing the five words he so often spoke as his feet touched onto the playground, "Come on Eddy, let's run!"

Run? My pudgy frame didn't run, it lumbered. Each step in the process was an ordeal for me. My feet seemed to punch the earth as if trying to create a dent and the other foot dragged slowly behind until maintaining an upright position necessitated its movement. Why would anyone want to do this on purpose? In contrast, Sam's feet seemed to tickle the earth as he effortlessly bound across the playground like a kid goat. I may have been the only one in my school looking forward to the bell ringing and recess being over. By the time we returned to class, my face was red, and I was a sweaty mess. Sam was invigorated. I needed a nap.

Sleepovers with Sam were always fun because his family lived in a rural part of town. In the back of their property was an old barn that we often explored, and his house was surrounded by large, furrowed fields. We had permission to explore whatever we wanted but it did come with a warning to be mindful of snakes and to stay away from them. I can't remember ever being allowed to stay over on a school night except for this single occasion. It was like any other sleepover, except our playtime was cut short as we had to get up early the following morning to catch the bus to school. My own home was only a brief walk from school, so taking the bus was another first-time adventure for me.

Sam and I were up early the following morning. We followed the normal school day routine of getting dressed and gobbling down a bowl of cereal before the two of us bolted out the door. Jeans with rolled up cuffs were the norm of the day, so I was careful to make mine as even as possible. After saying goodbye to Sam's mom, our next objective was to squeeze through a couple of strands of barbed wire fence and cross about two-hundred yards of plowed fields to arrive at our bus stop. It appeared to be a manageable distance, but I found walking through plowed fields to be immediately annoying. The rise and fall of the soil requires one to actually lift their feet off the ground to take a step. This seemingly unnecessary exertion was in absolute conflict with my slogging and dragging style of self-transport. To make matters worse, if I wasn't careful to lift my foot over the cusp of the furrow, dirt spilled into the neatly folded cuffs of my jeans. This was turning out to be a much bigger challenge than I suspected. I spotted a place near the halfway point and thought if I made it that far, I could stop, rest, eat part of the bagged lunch Sam's mom made for me and wait to be rescued.

After only a few steps into the plowed field, the entire scenario changed. There were about seven or eight other kids gathered ahead of us at the bus stop near the paved road when we heard them yelling, "The bus is coming!"

As our heads turned toward the end of the long rural road, sure enough, about a mile away we saw the familiar yellow bus heading in our direction. It was my worst nightmare because I knew what going to follow—the dreaded five words… "Come on Eddy, let's run!" If not for the peer pressure of my classmates, I may not have even attempted this ungodly sprint to the death. Sam was off to his usual fast start in what amounted to an unsanctioned race between myself and the fastest kid in my class—perhaps even the swiftest kid in the history of the third grade. He glided while I clomped over the furrows like a Clydesdale in a parade.

After only a half dozen steps into the ordeal, I felt something tugging at the cuff of my pants. The bus was coming, and I could not afford to lose additional ground, but I had to look to see what had attached itself to my cuff. It was discomforting enough to lift my feet off the ground in an effort to run, but now I had to manage to look back over my pudgy frame while maintaining forward progress. This is no easy task for a chubby kid. I glanced back and the only thing I could see was something long, black and narrow. My mind immediately flashed back to the warning Sam's mom had given us the day before and the only thing that registered in my brain was SNAKE! Each stride I made was being matched by this creature. I felt its tug upon me and was certain I was only milliseconds away from feeling its penetrating fangs and poison entering my body. I no longer cared about the bus, my classmates or Sam... I just wanted to live.

I don't know exactly at what point during the unsanctioned race that I passed Sam as it was all sort of a hypnotic blur. I ran past Sam, then continued past the bus stop and my cheering classmates too. The last thing I remember was hearing a scraping sound on the asphalt road and the thought coming to me, "snakes don't scrape." I came to my senses standing in the middle of the street. I turned, shook the long, narrow, black clothes hanger from my cuff and calmly walked to the door of the bus. My classmates were in such shock and awe that they stood in line and allowed me to board first. I sat in the coveted first seat next to the door and with quiet imagination, glowed inside with this new victory. It wasn't just a race. I had faced death and won.

The story, *Snakes Don't Scrape*, provides a humorous view and outcome of fear. This is not to diminish the power of fear, but to simply note that sometimes our fears are not poisonous vipers at all. Sometimes what we fear is only a metal clothes hanger that attaches itself to us and can be easily cast aside. That's the benefit of fear. It's a primal emotion that immediately engages our sense of survival. When we are faced with conditions that demand an immediate response and great energy, fear is the emotion utilized to maximize our chance of survival. The other side of fear is that it's debilitating as we seek to hide, shutting out all around us and quivering with uncertainty and insecurity. Fear is a tenacious, often volatile emotion. It's ever present to either aid or assault, but it is also an emotion we can learn to recognize and coexist with. C.S. Lewis, in *A Grief Observed*, writes, *"No one ever told me that grief felt so like fear. I am not afraid, but the sensation is like being afraid."*

As a memory aid, the first four obstacles to bereavement are identified by the acronym "FAIL" which stands for Fear, Anger, Isolation and Lethargy. By understanding and being aware of the pitfalls of grief recovery, we have a better chance of avoiding getting stuck in our recovery along the way.

Fear

Fear is one of the most common contributing factors to extended bereavement. By extended bereavement, I'm referring to a status within the processing of one's grief in which one becomes "stuck" and seemingly unable to progress any further. A more common expression used for extending one's period of bereavement is known as either prolonged or complicated grief. Complicated Grief is a term that may have originated with Dr. M. Katherine Shear, founder of the Center for Complicated Grief in Chicago. According to Dr. Shear, complicated grief is an existence identified as a state, "When someone is seemingly unable to make progress through bereavement."

Fear is a normal part of the grieving process. The loss of our loved one has resulted in life being put in a tailspin, and we are numb with pain while attempting to juggle finances, relationships, responsibilities, and a myriad of other issues. Anxiety is living in a perpetual state of fear and uncertainty. It can produce a sense of dread as though there's a threat at every turn, requiring us to stay in perpetual alert mode to deal with potential danger. It's exhausting to simply think about what that does to our mind and body. Here are some useful suggestions in dealing with fear and anxiety:

1. Identify what it is that you're afraid of. Face the fear.
2. Ask yourself the question, "Is it real?" Is it a clothes hanger or a snake? If it's a clothes hanger and we can accept that in our mind and emotions, problem solved. Sometimes, however, we can accept the fact that it's a clothes hanger in our minds, but we continue to feel like it's a snake. You're not crazy. I was at SeaWorld with my eight-year-old daughter many years ago. An exhibit there at the time was the stingray petting pool. I enjoy scuba diving whenever the opportunity avails, but there are certain underwater creatures I avoid with intent, one of them being a stingray. Although in my mind I knew the SeaWorld animal had its stinger removed, I couldn't bear to keep my hand in the water long enough to maintain extended contact or "pet" the stingray. My daughter, on the other hand, was so engaged with them that I thought she was going to end up in the pool with them. The threat was not real, but the feeling was.
3. Condition your thoughts. The acronym ANTS, or Automatic Negative Thoughts, was originally coined by Aaron Beck, M.D. and later popularized by the psychiatrist, Daniel Amen. The premise is that our minds display a cognitive bias, sometimes convincing us of something that isn't really true. As an example, I was going to a social function, and I knew a certain relative was going to be there. She usually brings up an uncomfortable subject and before we had arrived at the event, I convinced myself of the disaster that was to

come. It turned out to be a wonderful time, but I allowed my mind to create a false scenario that resulted in me initially being anxious and irritable. The solution to ANTS is to make PETS out of them, another acronym for Positive Empowering Thoughts. Once we're able to catch ourselves deep in negative thoughts, we can learn to replace them with positive thoughts and promises from scripture.

4. Sometimes it helps if we acknowledge the worst-case scenario. If this happens, what's the worst thing that would happen? I'd die and spend eternity in heaven? The Apostle Paul stated *"...for me to live is Christ and to die is gain."* Perhaps we'd lose a job, face embarrassment, or lose money. Are we able to look into the face of our fear knowing we can handle the worst outcome?

5. Get help. If the fear is real, i.e., if there's a mountain of bills and you're not an accountant, ask for help. If the fear is not real, and you know it's not real but can't get over the feeling of the threat and the resulting anxiety, find a local counselor who can guide you through the process. In the rare instance where the situation is real, seek help immediately from a pastor, counselor or social worker who can help with the problem.

Anger

One of the common mistakes people make after the loss of a spouse is dating too soon. I reiterate this to the group grief classes I lead on a consistent basis. It's not a good idea to make major decisions for a couple of years unless you have your back to the wall and are forced to sell the business or the primary residence. If you can stay where you are and work on your recovery, that's a good plan. If you feel so inclined, sell, donate, or give way whatever personal belongings you are able to comfortably depart with. But do not start dating right away. I've heard all the stories... "We fell out of love twenty years ago" "I know it's only been six months, but we've slept in separate beds for the last two years of our twenty-year marriage."

Have you ever taken the cover off a baseball to see what's inside? I did once when I was a kid and was amazed to discover that at the core is a hard rubber ball surrounded by, I'm exaggerating, eight-hundred miles of string. It took a week of my childhood to discover this. Marriage is like this. Through either death or divorce, when the cover comes off the marriage is over. Although it's legal to remarry the next day, the real you is the hard rubber core and you have twenty years of string to remove before you discover who you are apart from your former loved one. If you enter a relationship too soon, you're still wrapped in the string of the previous relationship. You're simply putting a new cover on the same baggage, expectations, and problems. Here's a story from my own list of failures to illustrate.

First Date Story

I had been single for several years when I met "Monique." She was an attractive, intelligent Christian woman with an outgoing personality and a great smile. She flirted with me, and I flirted back and suddenly we're going on a date. Admittedly, I made a couple of rookie mistakes. If I wasn't so distracted by her wit and charm, I would have asked more questions about her previous relationship. I had no idea that her long-term marriage had just ended and that I was her first post-divorce date. I also had no idea that her cheating husband left her for a twenty-something bimbo and that the two of them were off sailing the Caribbean. Only days prior, my date had finished moving from her beautiful home into a small condo. On the outside, she was an elegant, intelligent, and conversational woman. On the inside, she was that scary clown of horror films who is one evil chuckle away from making all your nightmares come true.

My second mistake was suggesting we go to her favorite restaurant for dinner. It's an innocent mistake, but one I will never make again. Monique was lovely when I picked her up. She greeted me with an affectionate hug and even gave me a quick kiss on the cheek when I met her at the door. Our conversation on the way to the restaurant was filled with smiles and several times she reached over to touch my hand as we talked. By all indications, this was going to be a spectacular first date. Conversation was easy, she was relaxed, comfortable, and seemed to enjoy physical contact with me. What could go wrong, right?

She looped her arm through mine as we entered her favorite restaurant. The maître d' immediately recognized her and lit up with a wide-faced smile. As his eyes and attention shifted toward me, his smile dropped, and his expression of gleeful welcome turned to confusion. It seemed odd but I ignored it. Regaining his composure, he quickly turned to Monique and with a restored smile, "Your favorite table, Madame?" Monique responded with a polite smile and a nod.

It was a busy Friday evening, and I was a little surprised when we were ushered past those waiting in line and immediately seated at a choice table. I didn't complain. I'm usually the guy seated next to the dumpster when I go to Taco Bell, so this was a nice change. The maître d' joyfully seated my date but lost his smile as soon as he finished assisting Monique into her seat. With a forced smile he threw my napkin in my lap from a distance as though he were tossing horseshoes and quickly disappeared. I initially felt a little slighted by his behavior but glanced up and Monique was smiling at me from across the candlelit table. I was instantly lost in her deep green eyes and couldn't be distracted by anything aside from her.

The conversation while waiting for our meals was light and playful—at one point she reached across the table and held my hand. I was having a great time. It wasn't until halfway through dinner that things went horribly wrong. No, it had nothing to do with the maître d' and everything to do with Monique. There was a slight pause in our conversation, and this is when she transformed into another person. Her arms became rigid as she tensely froze them in place, her hands gripping each side of the table. With clinched fists and her head slightly bowed, she looked up at me through the faint light of the candle. Her previously seductive and mesmerizing green eyes were now filled with anger. It was more than anger. She was experiencing full-on rage and all I could do was sit in helpless silence as she transformed into another persona. "You always say the same thing to me!" she growled.

At first her comments were soft and guttural but soon escalated and within seconds she was standing up, bent over, and yelling at me for how I have put her through hell. Her glossy eyes stared through me, and I quickly realized that I was nothing more than the crash dummy in this accident. It had become obvious I had been transformed into her former cheating husband. Needless to say, we were the star attraction for the scores of restaurant patrons. I quickly glanced around the room, perhaps looking for a friendly face to mouth the words, "Help me!" All I saw were scowls from other women who looked like they were ready to pitch in and help her beat the bad boy out of me. The men shook their heads and seemed to smile with relief that this wasn't happening to them. I was experiencing wide-eyed panic, frozen to my seat and unable to respond. Time seemed to pass in slow motion, one frame at a time. I'm not sure how long she lectured me for being a cheating son-of-a-donkey but when she had spoken her piece, she quietly sat down.

Once she was seated, I quickly turned and looked for the maître d' who had already prepared the check and was in the process of handing it to me. He looked at me with the first genuine smile of the evening.

Monique and I didn't speak until we were halfway home. To be honest, I was a little terrified of her at this point. She softly uttered an apology as she wiped away tears, explaining that her divorce had just finalized the week before and that she "got lost" in the situation. This restaurant was their long-term favorite and where we were seated, was special to them. As a couple, they had celebrated several birthdays and anniversaries at that same table—and now all it represented was the pain of his betrayal.

I never went out with Monique again but that's not to diminish the quality of person she is. It all boils down to bad timing and me making a couple of rookie dating mistakes. Needless to say, I've never been back to Monique's favorite restaurant. As a matter of fact, I try to completely stay away from that part of town these days.

If I do go there, you'll see me in my familiar seat next to the dump-ster at Taco Bell.

Here's the point of the story. Anger, bitterness and hurt don't magically disappear in a few months. Sleeping in separate rooms the final weeks and months of a relationship does little to resolve the accumulated hurts that took years to break down. It has nothing to do with the level of intimacy at the end of the previous relationship and everything to do with the love, memories, hurts and unmet expectations of the previous years shared. Each thread of the tight-ened ball of string must be unwound or we end up projecting and molding the new person into the one we recently departed from.

How do we deal with anger? First, learn to recognize it and consider another emotional response. I am not a golfer, but I do know that using a driver for a three-foot putt is probably not the best choice of clubs. Anger is a reaction to betrayal, unfair circum-stances, resentment, frustration, and a loss of control. In anger, we're asserting a dire effort to regain control, but anger is not an effective method of achieving that end. This is not to say we should stuff anger, simply replace anger as your autopilot response and release it in other ways. More effective ways of expressing anger are finding a safe place to yell and scream, engage in physical activity, meditation, walks in nature or punching pillows.

Monique's response at the dinner table was the result of stuffing her emotions. She obviously felt betrayed, belittled, and devastated by the accumulated losses of her marriage. Rather than process her grief and anger, she sought to pacify the pain by being comforted by another man. By not unwinding all the strings of her previous rela-tionship, she imposed them onto her date. Although she was initially able to appease the loss, the unprocessed pain surfaced with the familiarity of the surroundings, lost memories and the time invested in her husband. In the end, she was overwhelmed with the anger and rage of her unprocessed loss.

Isolation

Societal isolation is a problem as most Americans report being lonely. According to a Cigna survey of 20,000 adults, only 53% have meaningful daily contacts. With the loss of a loved one and grief added to the situation, we become vulnerable to a destructive form of isolation. This is further enhanced as we age, and our friends begin to pass. It almost feels as though our lives are being erased.

The Loss of a Childhood Friend

Recently, one of my childhood friends died and I had a strong emotional response to his death. After high school we drifted apart as geography and the pursuit of our individual dreams took us in different directions. I had only seen him once after high school and it had been decades since I saw him last. Despite that, I was profoundly impacted by the news of his death and posted the following on social media:

"One of my best friends from high school died yesterday. A classmate summed up my feelings well by expressing that a little piece of each of us died with him. It's true. Besides me, who is left to share the joint memories of our crazy adolescent adventures? I am now sadly alone as the sole keeper of these memories.

His death doesn't make me fear my own mortality as much as it threatens my present reality. It seems as though my life may not end harshly but fade away in increments as my friends and family slowly disappear in time. It's as stated in Psalm 103:15-16 "The life of mortals is like grass, they flourish like a flower of the field; the wind blows over it and it is gone, and its place remembers it no more." Will all I know and all I love fade from my life as each day passes? It triggers thoughts of my collective losses.

The benefit of grief is that it provides an opportunity to pause and reflect upon our life. Grief is the evidence of love now missing from our present reality. It's a time of contemplation and appreciation. I haven't seen my friend in decades, but I miss him. Seeing his name in print causes me to laugh aloud and sometimes I wonder how we survived as teenagers. I am grateful for the time and

*memories shared but I also feel more isolated by thoughts of a time and world
that no longer exists.*

Contributing to our isolation is what is identified by Dr. Ken
Doka, Professor of Gerontology at the Graduate School of The
College of New Rochelle, as "Disenfranchised Grief." Dr. Doka
defines this type of grief as: *"Grief that persons experience when they incur
a loss that is not or cannot be openly acknowledged, socially sanctioned or
publicly mourned."* I like this term because it so aptly applies to many
people with unresolved grief issues who have never taken the time
to recognize and process their pain.

The following list serves only as a sample of disenfranchised
grief, and some may spill over into other categories:

Lifestyle losses: the loss of a job, house, income, friends, or an
old familiar neighborhood.
Perceived marginal losses: miscarriages, former spouses, pets,
non-death injuries.
Stigmatized mechanism of death: suicide, homicide, drug overdose, HIV/AIDS.
Peripheral griever: a co-worker, childhood friend or ex-partner.
Stigmatized relationships: partner in an extramarital affair,
someone incarcerated, fan or admirer.
Stigmatized manner of grieving: the absence of an outward grief
response, overt expressions of grief.

Grief has many faces, but the emotional pain and sense of loss is
the commonality between the experiences. One can exhibit symp-
toms of grief from the loss of a job, divorce, issues of childhood
abuse, becoming an empty nester, or moving from an old familiar
neighborhood. We experience grief whenever we lose something we
love or have a strong emotional attachment to, whether that's a pet,
a friend or even a public figure that we've never met. Grief is simply
an emotional response to loss and with each loss we may experience
a deeper sense of disconnection and greater isolation.

What is the solution to isolation? Knowing the problem is half
the battle. If we close the curtains, lie in bed all day and close

ourselves off to the world, we could die. It will likely not be a sudden death but one in which we rot away from self-pity and self-destruction. We will live a tortured existence, recalling all the details and downfalls of each failure experienced and bath ourselves in guilt and remorse. It's a very slow, self-flagellating and exhausting death.

Rafting Story

I lived in Colorado for several years and while there, I enjoyed the annual white water rafting trips. Each year before we set out, the raft guide or captain would provide us with the three rules of rafting. The first rule was to stay inside the raft. The second rule was to stay inside the raft and the third, no surprise, was to stay inside the raft. The danger in rafting existed outside the raft so the simple admonition was to not go there. If, for some reason, one was to find themselves outside the raft, they were instructed to turn their bodies, with feet facing downstream, to protect their heads from impacting boulders and other debris. And with feet facing downstream, one was to listen to the commands of the captain.

Isolation during grief is similar to this scenario. The three rules of isolation are first, be around people. Second, be around people and as you may have guessed, the third is to be around people. All but a few close family members and friends will become scarce after the first few months. Everyone else will assume your needs are being taken care of or they secretly feel unsettled by your loss. More specifically, they either don't know what to say to you, or your loss forces them to think of their own mortality and potential for loss. They can't bear the thought of losing their own loved one and being around you reminds them of their own inevitable losses.

As the knocks on your front door dwindle, you need to be proactive. Join a group grief recovery class and make new friends there. Join special interest groups, community service groups, church groups, or volunteer with an organization you support. It may be a good idea to inform the leader of each group you join that you've suffered a recent loss and if you spontaneously cry or appear distraught, it's due to your loss and not a dynamic within the group.

Of course, many of us have full-time jobs and the break we receive from employment is often inadequate. We must work to survive, so we do. In that case, inform your employer that you're completely able to do your job but there may be times when you're sad, or perhaps disoriented—but it will pass.

If you find yourself outside of the raft, listen to the voice of the Captain. A benefit to isolation is discovered in the form of planned solitude. A regulated time alone with the specific intention of prayer and meditation is a great way to wade through the fog of grief and connect with God. Grief is often a cloud between us and God, but persist. He never leaves us or forsakes us. The Russian novelist, Fyodor Dostoevsky penned the words, *"The darker the night, the brighter the stars, the deeper the grief, the closer is God!"*

Lethargy

Lethargy is a condition characterized by fatigue, drowsiness, and an unusual lack of energy and mental alertness. It's a normal component of grief. But your body's fight, flight, or freeze response is meant for short durations. If it's activated all day, every day—it could overtax your nervous system. If you remain in this state for an extended period, it could lead to long-term mental and physical consequences. Remaining in a state of lethargy serves as a bog that slows down and can prevent us from progressing though grief. The following are suggestions as to avoid being captured in a mire of lethargy:

- Schedule a physical with your local physician.
- Remain physically active and exercise.
- Explore creative outlets.
- Express your emotions.
- Maintain a circle of friends and social groups.
- Eat healthy, drink healthy.
- Ask for help when needed.
- Make time to read scripture and pray.

Review

There are four primary components that negatively impact grief recovery. For the sake of clarity and to make it easy to remember, I utilized the acronym FAIL: Fear, Anger, Isolation and Lethargy. If you're stuck in the grief process and experiencing complicated or prolonged grief, it may be beneficial to review the possible reasons you FAIL.

Things to Know

*Always review and implement the previously suggested, "Things to Know" and "Things to Do" from the earlier chapters. Continue to add to your story. Keep writing, making notes and dating them.

1. Although there is no specific way to grieve and no timetable to follow, one must advance through the process by understanding the objectives and actively pursue that end.
2. People tend to fixate on the "why" or the reason behind the loss as though it's part of the grieving process. This can be an emotional trap that does nothing to bring the person back, allow you to feel better, nor does it resolve or process grief issues.
3. Scientists have found that grief, like fear, is a stress reaction, attended by deep physiological changes. Levels of stress hormones like cortisol increase. Sleep patterns are disrupted. The immune system is weakened. Mourners may experience loss of appetite, palpitations, even hallucinations. *They sometimes imagine that the deceased has appeared to them, in the form of a bird, say, or a cat. It is not unusual for a mourner to talk out loud—to cry out—to a lost one, in an elevator, or while walking the dog.* –C.S. Lewis

Things to Do

1. Check online for local group grief classes and commit to attending one. They are usually free except for perhaps the cost of the workbook. While on class, establish new friendships as there will be others in attendance that can relate to your loss and become a supportive friend.

2. Get help. Call the pastor of the church you attend or a nearby church and ask if there is a counselor on staff. Some churches provide counseling for a marginal fee and others offer a list of referrals to local skilled counselors.

3. Take inventory of your health; make an appointment to see a physician, throw out all the junk food in your panty and eat well, exercise, pray and meditate.

God hears our prayers—fragmented, reeking of pain and disoriented, God never leaves us. There's an old gospel song that utilizes the line, *"Tears are a language that God understands."*

Chapter 9
Adapting To A New Life

Situations appear overwhelming in the days immediately following the loss of our loved one when chaos prevails. Sometimes it's difficult to determine what's real and what isn't. We progress through grief by taking small, concerted steps in the right direction and by utilizing the tools and information contained in the previous chapters. At the same time, we're learning to steer clear of the obstacles and hazards, work through the pain of our loss, and redirect our efforts in a new environment. Finally, we catch a glimmer of hope and begin to entertain the thought that we're through the toughest part of our journey. Not to discourage you, but relapses are common. There will be days when you think all is well and the following day you'll be in shambles. Remember, recovery from a significant loss takes time. Save the victory lap for when you have more good days than bad and more smiles than tears.

The Soviet Submarine Story

Few people know this story as it never made it to the press or was talked about in a public forum—until now. As a seventeen-year-old teenager, my girlfriend and I saved the City of San Diego from a

Soviet invasion that could have resulted in the complete annihilation of "America's Finest City." Of course, this was several decades ago when a Cold War existed between the Union of Soviet Socialist Republics (USSR), better known as the Soviet Union, and the United States. At that time, cell phones were not commercially available and to make a telephone call, we had to find a telephone booth and place a dime into the slot to make a call. For younger readers, a dime is ten cents, and a phone booth is a small, closet-like structure with a permanently attached telephone for public use. It's stationery and attached by a cord. One must remove the hand-held device from the cradle, deposit a dime into the slot and physically dial a number using a rotary device. It requires a little patience as the caller must wait for a dial tone (a buzzing sound) before beginning to dial the number. There's no slot for a credit card and it doesn't recognize voice commands. I suppose this explanation dates me somewhat but if you think this is terrifying, I actually graduated from high school before hand-held blow dryers were invented.

Back to the story. I was a high school senior, out with my girlfriend on what began as a Saturday night date but had extended into the wee hours past midnight. We were sitting on the large rocks near the harbor shoreline of Shelter Island. If you're a San Diego local, you're probably familiar the stunning views that can be seen from the parking area immediately south of the Bali Hai Restaurant.

It was a warm, dark, moonless night with only a very slight breeze coming off the ocean. The lack of wind and boat traffic resulted in the water displaying a glasslike serenity, creating a mirror of the San Diego skyline that seemed to shimmer and dance in unison with its light of origin. The two of us were close enough to put our feet in water but were content dangling our feet inches above the small, pulsating waves that slurped near our feet. As our eyes feasted on the beauty of our surroundings, an object came into view in the middle of the channel. At first, we ignored it but the more we examined its shape and deliberate direction, it seemed suspicious—perhaps even threatening. The tone of my girlfriend's questioning changed from an innocent query of, "I wonder what that is?" to a more emphatic, "What is that thing?"

To place the situation in context, this was during an era when the entire world lived under the ongoing threat of mutual nuclear inhalation. We were two vulnerable teenage kids sitting out on the rocks by ourselves in the dark, and cell phones had not yet been invented. It was akin to being on a remote camping trip with everyone having a great time until a strange noise is heard in the forest. From that moment on, every snapped twig or rustle of leaves possessed the potential to be something with nefarious intent.

Although we could not see the object with any degree of clarity, its outline flickered into view with each rotation of the pulsating light emanating from North Island, on the other side of the harbor. The object resembled a swimmer's arm, fully extended with the hand pointed forward. One could even say it was like the grainy photos everyone has seen of the Loch Ness monster. We couldn't take our eyes off it. With our imaginative minds spinning with possible solutions, it was only a matter of moments before we both reached the same conclusion. It's a periscope! Sure, there was a U.S. Navy submarine base at the mouth of the harbor, but our boats never entered the harbor submerged. We looked at one another and almost in unison said, "It's a Soviet sub!"

As soon as we spoke the words, the periscope made a radical course change and was coming right toward us! It was almost as if they heard us. We scampered halfway up the rocks, laughing but admittedly scared. We had to call the police, but had no idea as to the location of the nearest phone booth or if we even had a dime to dial the operator. As the Soviet periscope edged toward us, we continued our climb but paused at the top of the rocks to take a glance back. The periscope was really getting close—too close. If it were a real sub, it would be crashing on the rocks by now. We paused once again but the new information didn't serve as ample enough a reason for my girlfriend to release her death grip on my arm.

Suddenly, I had a new revelation. I had recently watched a story on the news about the new, two-man subs. It was all making sense now and I blurted out, "It's a two-man sub!" I didn't think it was possible, but my girlfriend's grip on my arm tightened. Even if we survived, I was sure to lose a limb in the process. We assumed a quasi-sprint position at the top of the rocks, having determined that we could outrun the Soviet commandos with the head start we had. The periscope edged closer as we stood, hearts racing and in wide-eyed sprint mode. One final look back—there was a rustling sound and then—quack, quack! Neither of us spoke for a moment or two as the reality of what had just happened caught up to us. We slowly turned toward one another and laughed… and laughed and laughed. People in the nearby hotels may have thought us to be two crazy kids up past their bedtimes but little did they know that we had just saved the City of San Diego from a Soviet duck.

***

The moral of the story is, things are not always as they seem. Many times, the perceived threats and the things that go bump in the night aren't anything more than something being blown in the wind. It's easy to create more drama for ourselves than our lives need. Sometimes it's just a duck.

As we feel ourselves inching closer and closer toward our goal of adapting to our new life, a single incident can derail our progress and send us back to what feels like the starting point. These "ducks" are moments and situations called "triggers." Triggers are a normal part of the grief process. It's not an instrument of an enemy vessel that threatens our existence, it's simply a duck reminding us of what we lost. All our progress is retained in such instances, but our feelings jolt us back to those moments of acute emotional pain. This is normal. You have not failed and you're not starting over.

Many triggers are unique to the individual. Of course, we all share common triggers such as holidays, anniversaries, and birthdays but others catch us off guard and seemingly come out of nowhere. While standing in line at a grocery store, someone may be wearing the same cologne, the same item of clothing or even resemble your loved one. We can be on social media and see a photo of a vacation spot that we once visited, overhear someone speak a phrase, or eat a familiar food. Almost anything can trigger memories of our loss. Triggers are inevitable so if we can't eliminate them, we must learn to deal with them. But how do we do that?

Exercise patience. Acknowledge that triggers are unavoidable, they will come, but in time they will become less frequent and less intense. The problem we have in American culture is we want immediate results. During the delivery of our second daughter, I was bedside in the hospital, "coaching" my wife through the birthing process. She had dilatated to eight centimeters and was experiencing horrible contractions. My job was to verbally count the contractions to let her know how far into the wave of pain she was. If I correctly remember, the contractions lasted about thirty seconds and then there was a brief rest period before the next one began. During one very painful contraction, I was holding her hand and counting, one thousand one, one thousand two... and so on. At about one thousand fifteen, my mild-mannered wife looked at me with disheveled hair and a demonic stare, "Count faster, you idiot!" I felt horrible for her but could not contain my laughter. The nurse made me leave the room for a brief time but she too, was holding in the hilarity of the situation. I was fired from my coaching job for a few minutes but was allowed to return to see and experience the birth.

Counting faster does not speed up the pain of the process. We all follow the same painful route in grief and there are no quick fixes to speed up the clock. As with the birthing process, we know it's painful, but we can find relief in the knowledge that it's not forever, we will survive, and life will be better in a brief time.

Another strategy for dealing with triggers that arise is to come up with a plan. Rather than attempt to wing it and ride out the wave of emotional pain, we can preplan our response. For example, during holidays, we can make plans to spend time with family and friends. For those without connections to family, volunteering to serve is a good way to stay busy while enjoying and being supported by the company of others. For those random, out of nowhere triggers, determine what most effectively settles your heart and do that. For me, it was hiking. Pounding the turf and being in nature was a good way for me to expend energy while absorbing the beauty of my surroundings. As it was not always convenient to hike, a walk or bike ride achieved the same result. Others need to be around people or chat with a close friend. If you have a few close friends that are available on short notice, their company or conversation may be all you need. As a caution, do not utilize the same friend each time or you will burn them out. Even a close friend can only absorb so much of your pain before it begins to affect them. Also, make sure your "go-to plan" does not include alcohol or non-prescribed drugs, or you'll end up with more than one problem.

Finally, stick to the plan. Plans only work when they're carried out. In the days before cell phones, I was living in Pasadena and had a friend who lived in San Diego who was coming up for a weekend visit. I provided him with precise directions and told him the trip would take two and a half to three hours. He was a little paranoid about "L.A. traffic" but set out on the journey. I didn't hear from him until five hours later when he pulled over to call me from a phone booth (younger readers please refer to the explanation in the duck story). When he called, he said he had good news and bad news. The good news is that traffic was light, and he was making great time. The bad news was that he took a wrong turn and was a couple of hours away from Las Vegas, Nevada—in essence, great progress in the wrong direction. When triggered, exercise patience. We can't speed up time, but we can recognize it's a short-term obstacle. Develop a plan and stick to it.

Strike Out King Story

Little League Baseball was divided into two main categories when I was a kid: the nine and ten-year-olds played in the "Minors" and the eleven and twelve-year-olds played in the "Majors." For some reason, my dad and his drinking buddy thought it would be a good idea for me to play in the league with the big kids as a ten-year-old. It may not have been the best plan as a year or two in age makes a huge difference in performance. When I was at bat, the balls being thrown were like comets to me. Needless to say, I struck out a lot.

Before I get to the game, there's another person involved in the story. Rusty was my mom's friend. She was of Irish decent and had flaming red hair, accented with bright blue eyes. She stood all of five feet tall but was fearless. In her youth she worked for the circus as a high-dive performer. I remember seeing pictures of her standing atop a diving board that I can only guess to be about twenty-five feet above a small pool of water. Dad didn't like her because she wouldn't allow him to bully her. I liked her for exactly that reason, plus I thought she was an interesting person.

On one Saturday, toward the end of our baseball season, my team was playing in the second of the three games scheduled that day. There must have been over a hundred people in the stands, including Rusty. We were in second place, but that ranking was being challenged as we were behind in the game. At a critical time in the contest when we had a chance to win, it was my turn at bat. The announcer spoke my name over the sound system, "Now at bat, Eddy Keebler," resulting in a collective groan from the crowd.

One of the dads couldn't contain himself, stood to his feet and spoke in a loud voice, "Come on coach! Get that kid out of there! All he does is strike out!"

I suppose the man didn't notice that Rusty was sitting about eight rows down from him. She jumped to her feet, pointed at the outspoken man, and spoke in angry voice, "Shut up and sit your ass down!" The crowd chuckled with amusement and after a brief pause, she added, "He's going to hit a home run!" She stared at the man until he sat down. There were a lot of eye rolls and polite smiles but no one in the crowd believed her prophetic claim could come true.

In typical fashion, I approached the plate with great intimidation. I stood and watched the first two strikes go by without attempting more than a prolonged look. But I was determined to swing on the third pitch. I don't remember much about the pitch other than feeling my bat connect with the ball. I thought I hit a foul ball but was elated to have done that much. As I looked up, I saw the ball in fair territory, and I was nearly doing cartwheels as I ran toward first base. I hit a fair ball! It didn't even matter if the other team caught it for an out—I actually hit the ball and didn't strike out! In the moment that followed, I tracked the ball as it lifted into the outfield. This was a dream come true. Again, I didn't care if a fielder caught the ball, the fact that I hit it into the outfield was reward enough. I continued to watch as the ball drifted deeper and deeper into center field until it finally disappeared over the fence. It was a home run! I was in a state of wide-eyed astonishment as I ran toward second base. My friend, Barry, played second base for the other team and he reached out to shake my hand. After I shook his hand, I pulled my hat down over my face and cried all the way to home plate. Rusty's impossible prophecy had come true.

Here's the point of the story. In grief, and life in general, you'll have options as to what kind of people surround you. It's easy to gather those who commiserate with your loss and who will cry and share their stories of pain with you. Many are wonderful souls but in a time of great loss and devastation, look for someone who sees the gold in you. Some are blessed with a gift of encouragement and will continue to remind you of your strengths and value. During great loss, it's easy to retreat into ourselves and find little value in the rubble. Find that person who is ready to stand up and proclaim you're a home run hitter.

How do we find people like this? Pray and wait. An odd dynamic frequently occurs in the aftermath of grief in that people you think will be with you through the process end up abandoning you and others come out of nowhere to be your strongest allies and sources of comfort. Those who exit your life are not uncaring, they are often so haunted by your loss that they are unable to handle the grief. They distance themselves from you because being around you often results in them feeling vulnerable. What if they lost a spouse, sibling, parent, or child? The thought is unbearable. When they're around you, they don't know what to say or do to make you feel better. They feel helpless, useless, and afraid so they fade from your life. But don't worry—those on the fringe of your life and people you have yet to meet, will often appear.

Reseda Traffic Guy

On January 17, 1994, at 4:31 a.m. a 6.7 magnitude tremblor hit the Los Angeles area in what is known as the Northridge Earthquake. It hit with a resounding jolt that roused even the heaviest sleepers and sent people scampering outside into the darkness of the early morning. Those near the epicenter described the experience as the sound of a train coming through the house. Glass from windows, dishes and fragile containers covered the floors of most rooms and the brick walls surrounding many homes had collapsed. One couple who had rented a room in a nearby hotel, unintentionally surfed the wreckage and destruction of the surrounding building on their mattress, finally settling aground outside on a bank of succulents. They were still clinging to their mattress and completely unharmed.

In the hours immediately following the earthquake I was driving toward Reseda Blvd. and standing in the middle of one of the busiest intersections in the San Fernando Valley was the Reseda Traffic Guy. The sun was just coming up and he stood there directing traffic amid the chaos. He was disheveled in appearance, standing in his bare feet, and wearing only shorts and a casual short-sleeved shirt. He looked as though he had just tumbled out of bed. Traffic lights, power, and communications were all down. Chaos surrounded the man as panicked people scurried about attempting to check on relatives and gather what supplies were available. After-shocks rolled through the Valley as we waited in line to pass. The tremblors were visible as the asphalt road rose and sank like a wave in the ocean. It didn't phase the Reseda traffic Guy as he maintained his post and directed traffic throughout the day. I checked back with him later in the day as the sun bore down on the hot asphalt. There was a pile of flip flops, and several sodas and bottles of water surrounding him as motorists leaned out of their vehicles and placed them at his feet. He was just an ordinary guy who was compelled to help. The need to help screamed inside his soul and he looked for an opportunity to do something, anything, to help ease the chaos and suffering of others. To me, he was the Reseda Traffic Hero. I worked disaster relief for a few years and have been a hospice chaplain for several years. In each disaster or loss, there's always a common person who puts on their hero hat and selflessly goes to work.

When we are in moments of despair, God sends heroes to stand with us. Pray and wait with the assurance that they will be compelled to reach out to us. We may even decline or push them away the first time, but be mindful that they will come. Allow them to do what God has gifted them to do and accept their help.

Along the way, we'll run into both heroes, idiots, and everyone in-between. The idiots are not purposely malicious, they are generally ill-informed individuals who don't know what to say or do, yet they feel it's necessary to impart a word of advice or "wisdom" to us. Most often, it's a statement like, "Well, they're better off now" or "I know exactly how you feel" or even "It's all for the good" which may be true in light of our view of eternity but it's not something to say to someone at a funeral. To deal with such individuals, I simply nod and smile while thinking, "You're an idiot." It probably only applies to the individual at that moment, but that's how I cope with unsolicited wayward comments. Jesus handled the situation so much better when He stated, "Father, forgive them for they know not what they do."

In the end, grief recovery is not so much a journey as it is a direction. It's not like a road trip that we can plan from San Diego to Boston, it's a path without a firm destination. We begin at heartbreak and move away from it until we can cope and adapt to our new surroundings. We learn how to manage our lives without our loved one. We don't stop missing or loving them, we simply come to a place where we can look up and appreciate beauty, opportunity, and a future without them.

Review

In the Duck Story we discussed that not everything is as it appears during times of grief. We can be at the top of the world one day and be completely devastated the next. You haven't failed. It's normal. The ducks are triggers that are manifested on key days or ignited by reminders of our loss. We must anticipate and plan a response to triggers. Nothing speeds up the process, so we must have the resolve to keep moving in the right direction and stick to the plan. In the process of executing the plan, look for encouragers, who believe the best in us, and will support us. God always sends heroes.

We have now completed nine chapters. Gather your notes and comments from the previous chapters and update your story. You may never show what you've written to anyone, but it will serve as a record to demonstrate your growth from the depths of despair to where you are now. Your story should reflect your thoughts on God and the afterlife as well as demonstrate an idea as to a direction and plan you intend to follow. Your story should display elements of self-examination, your personal struggles, and how God has intervened in your life. You should understand forgiveness and reflect that in your story. Stories record failures and victories. Identify what struggles you are facing now and how you intend to avoid getting stuck.

Things to Know

*Always review and implement the previously suggested, "Things to Know" and "Things to Do" from the earlier chapters. Continue to add to your story. Keep writing, making notes and dating them.

1. When terminally ill patients get close to transition (days, weeks, or months away) they sometimes see visions of people they know who are deceased. These visions are distinctly different from hallucinations as hallucinations are typically confusing, the details are difficult to remember, and they are sometimes violent. Visions have a calming effect on patients, and they often can recall details.

2. Departure language is when someone nears the end of life, and they seem to be eager to go somewhere important. The details are often unclear, but they have a certain fancy gown they want to wear, or they want to make sure their shoes are shined. Some express thoughts

of being picked up in a fancy car and taken to a banquet.

3. NDE or Near Death Experiences have dramatically increased since the use of automated external defibrillator, or AED's. People who experience this phenomenon are often able to recall people, conversations and details of events that occurred while they were listed as officially deceased.

Things to Do

1. Make a plan for unexpected triggers.
2. Have a conversation with family as to what to do with your departed loved one's clothes and personal items. Do not allow anyone to rush you into a decision but when you're ready, discuss your plans.
3. Join a new church small group or a club that is the focus of a shared interest. Think of ways to be around people.

"Your life does not get better by chance, it gets better by change."

—Jim Rohn

Chapter 10
Grief Illustrated

Anne's Suicide

Anne had a long-term bout with fibromyalgia and chronic fatigue syndrome, which eventually led to her becoming addicted to prescription pain meds. I admit to being ignorant about the addictive power of pain medications and made the mistake of assuming she was being responsible in her consumption of the pills prescribed.

On this particular evening, it seemed like the usual routine—she always became tired early and went to bed before me, so I thought nothing was different when she retired early for the night. About an hour after she went to bed, I heard a noise coming from upstairs that sounded like something had dropped onto the floor. I listened intently for a few seconds and there was no other noise or call for help, but thought it best to check on Anne anyway. I opened the bedroom door to discover her body on the floor with her feet still tangled in the sheets. She was conscious but nearly incoherent. Her eyes were open, but she was obviously dazed and desperately waving one arm at me in an attempt to keep me away. As I reached for the bedside phone to call 9-1-1, she was able to land her arm on mine and clutch onto my wrist with her hand. She attempted to say, "No!" but it came out more as a grunt than a clearly defined word. I used my free hand to gain control of the phone and was communicating with the dispatcher as she fell unconsciousness. I carried her downstairs and held her until the paramedics arrived.

Once at the hospital, I couldn't see Anne right away, so I took advantage of the break to call her family and church. We had recently moved and the church we attended was one that Anne had attended for many years, but one at which I was a newcomer. By the time I was able to see Anne, she was still unconscious, and her mouth was now encircled with charcoal. The medical team had done everything they could do up to this point and it was now a matter of waiting to see if she was strong enough to make it. By the time her sisters arrived, nothing had changed. It would take several hours for the charcoal to work and for her body to process the drugs already in her system.

Anne's siblings seemed oddly irritable toward me. I thought they would express more compassion at a time like this, but their questions and comments seemed suspicious in nature. To everyone who knew her, Anne was a gregarious, life-of- the- party persona that everyone loved. I suppose their rationale begged the question, why would someone like this attempt suicide? The last time everyone saw her she was her normal, funny, happy, and carefree self. The unspoken question to me was, "What did you do to her?" Anne's long-term friends from her church showed up and displayed equally odd behavior. When I entered the room they were gathered in, everyone became silent, and no one attempted to offer so much as a greeting or acknowledgment of my presence. Then, of course, there was the police. They had to do their job and I understand that, but it did seem as though they probed way too deeply into motives where I had merely acted responsibly in saving my wife's life.

By morning Anne was conscious and determined to be in good health, displaying no permanent brain damage or side effects from her incident. Although greatly relieved to have my wife back and in good health, I continued to have to contend with a rather cool attitude from her family and friends in the months that followed. It was not until Anne's second suicide attempt six months later that people caught on to the fact that the suicide attempts were completely on Anne's initiative. After I saved Anne's life a second time from a deliberate overdose, these same people told Anne to tell me that they were sorry for accusing me of anything. I'm easy to extend forgiveness toward others, as I know that holding any kind of grudge or resentment impacts only me. I can be gracious, kind, and even generous to people that have wronged me, but I do have a choice as to who I allow close to me.

Few realize the sacrifices made by the healthy caregiver until they've experienced it. It's more than simply accepting the workload and domestic responsibilities of two people, there is a low-grade anxiety that that percolates under the added tasks of appointments, medications, researching alternative treatments and a hundred other things that fall in one's lap. It's a labor of love but to endure it, one must look beyond the present reality. My beautiful wife was sleeping in a separate bedroom, our relationship had been platonic for several years and my reward was to become the object of her pain, criticism, and anger. The situation left me socially isolated and with no life of my own. To cope with the circumstances, I kept reminding myself that this was not a true reflection of the sweet woman I married, but a desperate and pain-ridden version of her.

Over the course of the next few years, Anne tried to end her life a total of five times. After her fifth attempt, I petitioned the state agency to have Anne held for additional treatment and they begrudgingly allowed her ten days beyond the normal seventy-two-hour period. I spent time with her daily, but it broke my heart when she begged me to let her end treatment early and come home. After she was released, she initially complied with counseling and met with a specialist on a regular basis, but it quickly became obvious to me that she was merely going through the motions. The drugs she consumed kept her either asleep or groggy eighteen to twenty hours a day and her few conscious hours were filled with discomfort. Life appeared to be nothing but a painful routine, and in her mind, all had become hopeless. From her perspective, death was her only escape. I suspected that the drugs were killing her, but I couldn't convince her to attempt treatment without them. Her sixth suicide attempt was successful.

How does one grieve suicide? It's different than a normal death in that it feels as though one mourns in solitude. In my situation, Anne's eventual suicide was more akin to experiencing an anticipated death, such as a known terminal illness combined with the sudden death it was. As guilty as I feel for mentioning it, I was relieved when she was finally free from pain. I'm also nearly ashamed to admit that I wanted a normal life for myself, to feel loved, appreciated, and valued. I wanted to enjoy the physical touch of the one I loved, to enjoy her presence and simply share a meaningful connection. In the final years, Anne's pain had become all-consuming and much of her dissatisfaction with life was directed toward me. I, too, was angry because I wanted a longer, healthier life for her and I was angry with her for not trying harder to break away from her devastating drug addiction.

In the end, regardless of the manner of loss, we still must complete the tasks of grieving. One must face the reality that those we love are not coming back, and acknowledge that grief is both a cognitive and emotional process. We heal and gain awareness by actively coming to a more complete understanding of what we are experiencing while making deliberate choices to advance ourselves through the process. We learn to confront the reality of our loss and restructure our thoughts regarding our loved one. We face our loss with vulnerability and honest emotions while trusting God to love us and heal our wounds. By God's grace, we can forgive those that blamed and falsely accused us while receiving forgiveness ourselves. The major difference in grieving suicide is that it feels as though you're processing your pain alone behind a curtain of shame.

It's been several years since her death, but I still think of Anne often. I can still remember the feel of her hand in mine and the contour of her body in my arms. I can close my eyes and envision her shoulder-length hair and the expressiveness of her eyes. One eye was slightly different in color than the other—no one would know that unless they were allowed the intimacy of staring into her beautiful eyes for several moments. She had a mischievous smile, and I always knew if she wasn't up to something, she was thinking it. We used to sit in the front row of the movies and put our feet up on the railing. When the theater went dark before the feature film began and before everyone's eyes adjusted to the dark, she leaned over and demanded a kiss. It wasn't a quick peck either. She knew that a passionate kiss in public made me a little nervous and I think that's part of the reason she enjoyed it. These are moments that make me smile when I am reminded of her.

On our tropical island honeymoon, we discovered a restaurant that catered to locals on the backside of the island. As newlyweds, the home crowd treated us like royalty but when the music and dancing started, I was horrified. I'm not musically inclined and, didn't know how to dance—in fact, I was intimidated by the thought of even attempting to dance. Admittedly, at first I refused, but a female travel writer was next to us and whispered in my ear, "This is a moment she will remember for the rest of her life. Don't screw this up!"

I think Anne heard at least part of what she said. My new bride looked deeply into my eyes and whispered into my other ear, "Trust me. I'll make you look good."

I've been sky diving, hiked wilderness trails, been on a dozen white-water rafting trips and been within a few feet of sharks while scuba diving—none of this prepared me for the dance floor. Completely sober and with knees trembling she led me to a cozy part of the room. I held onto her like a frightened child while letting her guide me through the steps. "Now lift your hand above my head," and as I did, she spun with grace and magically reappeared in my arms. I was actually having fun. Among all the wonderful things that we experienced on the trip, I will never forget dancing with her.

Anne's health began to deteriorate in the years that followed, and our honeymoon ended up being the single time we danced together. Oddly, since her death, I've taken up ballroom dancing as a hobby. I'm not very good at it but I enjoy it, and sometimes I think of Anne and her statement, "Trust me. I'll make you look good." This is how I choose to remember her, and this is where she resides within me. If I dwell on her death, I can allow a wave of grief to crash over my head but given the choice, I'll opt for calm waters. I choose, in my present life, to adjust and adapt to the person and the life I have apart from her. I'm an individual now but Anne will always have a presence and live within the framework of my memories. She now dances with a wide smile in eternity and in my divine imagination, I can see her there.

Debbie's Story

Tomorrow it will be one year since I lost my husband. When this day comes, it doesn't feel right to just let it pass by unnoticed, but you don't throw a party to celebrate... it's a day that I hope those around me will understand why I am quiet and why my smile won't be as visible as it normally is. It's a day I will reflect on all the time. I shared with him all of me and still hold those memories close to my heart. It's been a tough year dealing with Escrow people, closing his business, DMV paperwork, taxes, making big decisions with the hope he would approve, and much, much more. I stood up to the lawyer for what I felt was right and I completed tasks I never thought I could. Some say I am a strong woman for being able to handle all of this, but tackling all these things kept me from thinking too much about missing him. So here I sit a year later, most of the estate work is complete which means I have extra time on my hands... and now I grieve. I will always love you, Bob. Thank you for loving me and for all the memories... rest in peace, babe.

Connie's Story

My "Grief Journey" started when my husband Dave passed away very suddenly and unexpectedly from Covid-19 complications on August 8, 2021. One day he got sick and 17 days later he was gone. He was hospitalized during his illness, and the hospital did not allow me to be with him until after he had passed away. That day forever divided my life from, "Before Dave to After Dave." The grief that day felt like a tsunami washing over me and carrying me out to the deepest depths of the ocean. I felt bruised, battered, and beaten, soaked by the flood of my own tears. The next wave hit me like an earthquake that shook the core of my being, leaving me shaken, unsteady and feeling like my husband had been ripped from my flesh. What God had joined together and made one flesh had been ripped apart! I was trying to live, move and navigate my life with half of my flesh gone like an amputee. The strong woman I thought I was had shattered into a thousand pieces on the floor. I felt like I was living with a scream trapped inside of me. My heart was like broken glass and felt like the pieces of glass were a lump in my throat. I felt raw, unstitched, and bleeding with a pain so deep I truly did not believe I would survive it. BUT God!

The day I left the hospital after saying goodbye to my husband's lifeless body, I heard God say to me in my mind, this is where the rubber meets the road as a Christian! Do you really believe everything you have said you believe? And that is when my real journey of grief and faith in God began.

To be honest, the journey has been brutal and horrific! It has been an incredibly arduous journey! After 45 years of walking with God I had to step out in true faith and learn to live the scriptures, not just merely quote them.

*Would God never leave me or forsake me? (Heb. 13:5)
*Was God faithful? (Psalm 33:4 & Deut. 7:9)
*Can I do all things through Him? (Phil 4:13)
*Will He direct my path? (Jer. 29:11)
*Will He give me more than I am able to bear? (1 Cor. 10:13)
*Can I walk through this valley of the shadow of death and have no fear? (Psalm 23)
*Does He heal the brokenhearted and bind up their wounds? (Psalm 147:3)
*Will He send His Angels to protect me? (Psalm 91:11)

Did I really believe the promises of scripture? And what I learned about God humbled and amazed me. He fulfilled every promise in His word. He wanted me when I was broken, bleeding, battered and shattered, and He was going to make me whole again. When I thought I had lost all hope, God revealed to me that He is "My Living Hope" and He lives inside of me. Yes, God is still writing my story, He has closed a few chapters, but He is writing the rest. I just have to BE Still and trust in His plan without trying to grab the pen away.

Barbara's Story

Michael, was my husband of almost 38 years when he went to Heaven. I thank God every day that I was given the strength to fulfill my wedding vows to care for him during his last 4 months of his life. I thank God that Michael was in my life for almost 40 years.

This is my view of grief:

TORTUROUS PAIN, beyond my imagination. The psychological becomes physical. Like needles penetrating the skin—so sensitive, I will break like glass if a feather slightly grazes my skin.

ALONE. Becoming alone after our minds and bodies were inter-connected is brutal. Now, I am just one. Now, all decisions—small or large—become daunt-ing. Again, the mental becomes physically exhausting. Making daily decisions like —what to eat, what time to get out of bed or feed the cats... Everyday life is debilitating.

LOST. I never imagined I would have to find myself. I was fine the way we were. LOST! Who am I now? What shall I do with my life?

GOING CRAZY. I was always the sensible one. I thought I was sane dealing with everyday life, easy-peasy. Now, life is complete madness, a roller coaster of sanity and a little deranged.

MEMORIES. I still miss Mike every day. All the above is less painful, tears flow less often. I'm slowly developing a life without him (very slowly). Our memories feel like a puff of smoke. Did this really happen? Some days I fall apart. I consider these times normal.

My prayer that eases my loss:

Dear God,
Thank you for the strength and privilege to take care of my precious love, Mike.

Thank you for all the years you gave him to me. Through him, I was given love and lessons about life that will stay with me forever. Laughter, smiles, compassion, enjoying life every day, loving everyone you meet, without judgment. In Jesus name. Amen.

Matt's Story

I can't process the fact that she's gone. After 23 years together, I can rationalize the fact that she's no longer with me, but Dana is deeply engrained into my core. I can't seem to stop verbalizing her name and expecting her to answer. I initiate texts and calls to her without thinking and sometimes I drive by places we've spent time together. Is it possible this is all a bad dream that I'll wake up from and the next time I drive by, she'll be there? The next time I roll over in bed and reach for her, will I feel her next to me? We were a team—I fixed things and did the heavy lifting while she charmed the birds from the sky and made me feel comfortable with people. Now I just want to be alone. At the same time, I do like it when people make an effort to check on me. I do appreciate it. I just don't know how to show it very well. Dana did that for me.

My emotions are all over the place. It was so sudden… a tire on the highway. I know God is with me but it's difficult for me to feel his presence or love. Honestly, I'm not at a place where I can think about God much. I don't blame God for Dana dying, but God seems distant and being around church people makes me feel awkward. I pray, watch sermons on TV and intend to join a small group soon. I'm trying. Really, I know she would want me to have a life, but I miss that about her too.

Review

Grief is experienced in many forms. Someone who is grieving for a loved one who is terminally ill with a long-standing illness often experiences anticipatory grief. It's a process of gradually letting go but the impact of their death still hits with force. Such individuals struggle with feeling relieved that it's finally over, that their loved one is no longer suffering and that they can have a life of their own. Sadly, we feel guilty for feeling relieved.

Two primary categories of grief are prolonged or sudden grief.

Prolonged grief is as described above whereas sudden grief is something entirely unexpected. Disenfranchised grief is ascribed to what one feels when processing the loss of someone or something that is not entirely acceptable, is awkward or not acknowledged by society in general. Examples are suicides, the death of a former lover, pet, or an old neighborhood. Incomplete or delayed grief is when one does not, or feels they cannot, process their loss. "Stuffing" grief manifests itself later in what is often demonstrated as angry and/or self-destructive behaviors. The stories mentioned in this chapter display the various types of grief and responses of those suffering loss.

Things to Know

*Always review and implement the previously suggested, "Things to Know" and "Things to Do" from the earlier chapters. Continue to add to your story. Keep writing, making notes and dating them.

1. Approximately 70% of Americans have pets and the loss of a pet can be as devastating to someone as the loss of a person.
2. Over 48,000 people die from suicide each year in the United States. Approximately 80% are male, and the largest group represented are seniors over 85 years old.
3. A few ways to help those who are grieving is to deliver prepared meals, offer time to listen or to run errands, mow lawns or help with household chores.

Things to Do

1. Join a local group grief class. There are nationwide and local organizations that offer classes free of charge except for the cost of materials.
2. Check with local churches who have a staff pastor who offers a free session or two to discuss your situation. The

pastor will be able to direct you to local resources in your area.

3. Check online communities where people gather to share stories and resources.

"Though our feelings come and go, God's love for us does not."

— C. S. Lewis

Chapter 11
Near Death Experiences And Deathbed Phenomena

Izzy's Curse

My grandmother's name was Clara, but we only knew her as Maw Maw. As with many families, I'm certain the name is a derivative of the eldest grandchild's attempt to pronounce the word, "grandma." Rather than wrestle with the linguistic challenge, the more affectionate and common name stuck. This brief story was passed on to me by my cousin Rodney, but for the sake of clarity since the context deals with Maw Maw's early life, I'll simply refer to her as Clara.

As with many Southern women, born at the turn of the twentieth century, Clara was a young bride at fifteen years-old, and had three children before she reached her twentieth birthday. Unfortunately, my biological grandfather abandoned the family and left her living with her father during a very difficult period in American history. After obtaining a divorce from her first husband, Clara captured the eye and affection of a man in the neighborhood—a Frenchman by the name of Isadore Fayard or "Izzy" as he was known.

Their relationship slowly started as Izzy simply dropped off groceries for Clara and her children at the doorstep. In time, a relationship developed and eventually the two married. Izzy was a good man, deeply moral and honest. When walking down the street, he was known to cross over to the other side rather than walk in front of a bar or dance hall. Unfortunately, while working on an oyster boat, he slipped on a grated deck grill and cut his leg to the bone. The surface wound healed but he was too stubborn to submit to any further medical treatment. One day, years later, a blood clot detached from the damaged bone and resulted in heart failure. He died at thirty-eight years old. During the time he was ill, Izzy repeatedly told Clara, "If I die, I don't want you to ever go to those pool rooms, bars or dancing halls." Then Izzy gave her a stern warning, "If you ever go to those places, I'll come back and haunt you after I die!" I think Izzy knew that Clara, who was married at 15, desired a taste of freedom and longed for an adolescence she never had.

After Izzy's death, as he suspected, Clara sought out the excitement of the dancing halls and bars that she never had the opportunity to experience in her youth. But Izzy wasn't forgotten. Almost weekly she visited his grave, clearing it off and then sitting directly over his burial spot. Of course, properties along the Gulf Coast have very high water tables and gravesites are notorious for instability. As Clara sat on top of the grave during a visit, the ground under her gave way and she began to sink into the shallow cavern. As her body sank into Izzy's burial plot, only a few inches, she screamed out in horror, "No, Izzy! No!" She was certain that Izzy was coming back to keep his promise of haunting her for her misdeeds.

Near Death Experiences (NDEs)

I was in my late twenties when I experienced the dream of Heaven detailed in a previous chapter. Although Anne and I received enormous comfort and encouragement from the dream, we seldom mentioned it to others because it seemed too mystical. When I did share the experience, people politely smiled and nodded as though I were describing an alien encounter with a being from another planet. But rather than allow other's reactions to invalidate my experience, I chose to investigate the matter further.

At the time of my baby daughter's death, the only research I could find related to this phenomenon was Raymond Moody's book, *"Life After Life."* In 1975 when the book was first published, the terms "near-death experience" and "deathbed phenomena" or "deathbed visits" did not exist. Naturally, despite Dr. Moody's scholarly credentials, the book was highly controversial, heavily criticized by those outside of the faith community and treated with suspicion by many inside the church. Several years later, however, new research has largely substantiated his conclusions.

"Life After Life" was an in-depth qualitative study on the near-death experiences (NDEs) of 150 patients. No two people had an identical experience, but of the fifteen components of afterlife markers that Moody identified, "very many" according to Moody, reported experiencing eight to twelve of them. Additionally, no single individual experienced all the elements of a NDE but nearly all of those examined held some aspects in common. The more consistent elements of an afterlife experience include the following:

- An overwhelming feeling of peace and well-being, and freedom from pain.
- A sensation of being located outside one's physical body.
- Floating through a dark place, sometimes within a tunnel.
- Being attracted to an irresistible light.
- Feeling the presence, having an encounter with, and/or communicating with another being from the light.
- Witnessing or "watching" an instantaneous visual review of one's past.
- Experiencing ethereal, otherworldly beauty involving the senses.

Naturally, when I read Dr. Moody's book twenty years after it was published, I was astonished to discover the similarities between a NDE and the dream I had. It served to validate my experience while deepening a greater curiosity on the topic within me.

The most blaring question is; why is there so much resistance, even within the Christian community, to acknowledging a near-death experience? Is it because we hear so few sermons and teaching on the afterlife, or is it because modern Western society has become somewhat immune to any experience outside the perception of our natural senses? Perhaps it's a combination of both. Dr. Moody's *"Life After Life"* includes a Preface written by Dr. Melvin Morse, an acclaimed pediatrician whose works include research of NDEs with children. Dr. Morse observed that for thousands of years, humans accepted death as a natural part of life but that a brutal evolution in our attitudes concerning death occurred at the turn of the last century. He goes on to state, "Death became unnatural, dirty, medicalized, and hidden from the public view. Whereas most people died at home in the 1800s, by the mid-twentieth century most people died in hospitals."

It's true—modern society insulates, separates, and medicates us from the experience of death. It is with noble intentions that medical facilities and elderly care institutions make an individual's life as comfortable as possible before we take our final breath. Once our loved ones have passed, they are then hidden from view until they are either dressed up or reduced to the ashes contained within a stylish urn. At every stage in the process, both the deceased and their surviving loved ones are shielded from as much discomfort as can be afforded. It's a luxury that did not exist in history until less than a century ago.

The objections from the scientific community to Dr. Moody's work included assertions that NDEs could easily be dismissed as the result of hallucinations or brain pathology. Others speculated that NDEs were either drug induced, a manifestation of temporal lobe epilepsy, or even the widespread release of a chemical called glutamate. These explanations held some ground until a study was published in 2004 by Dr. Peter Fenwick of the acclaimed Institute of Psychiatry at Kings College, London.

Dr. Fenwick gave a lecture that summarized his thirty years of research in the field of NDEs and in this presentation, revealed the results of his scientific findings. Based on a survey of 450 participants, 98% of whom had never heard of NDEs and had no preconceived notions about them, the group largely described the same or similar elements as noted in Dr. Moody's 1975 research.

"The phenomena reported during NDEs included 66 percent who reported an out-of-body experience, 76 percent pastoral landscapes, 38 percent seeing deceased friends and relatives, 12 percent life reviews, 24 percent a barrier of some sort, and 72 percent a decision to return."

Of those responding to the poll, approximately one-third of them were receiving drugs at the time of their NDE, in effect eliminating drug inducement as a catalyst for near death phenomenon. This holds true with death bed visions as well in that the great majority of those who report such sightings, are not under the influence of medication.

The "temporal lobe epilepsy" objection was introduced by Willoughby Britton and Richard Bootzin's study in which they suggest that near-death experiences are a manifestation of this condition. Others have quoted their work and used the Britton-Bootzin study as a reference, perhaps without realizing that the authors of this theory do not deal with epilepsy daily and lack a comprehensive understanding of this dynamic. For those epileptologists who work exclusively in the field, Dr. Fenwick states, "...all agree that on one thing—near death experiences are not temporal lobe epilepsy."

Another theory that some espouse as an explanation to near death experiences is the change in brain chemistry during cerebral anoxia. This is when the heart stops and there is no oxygen supply to the brain. There is a rampant release of the chemical glutamate that promotes widespread nerve stimulation, resulting in a chaotic firing in the brain cells that chemically can be compared to ketamine, a street drug that produces a feeling of contentment, creativity, and other pleasant effects. The downfall of this theory is that when ketamine was used in some studies (Evengy Krupitzky and Alexander Grienko, 1997) it produced similar effects to NDEs but with varied and inconsistent results. NDEs follow a much more specific pattern, allowing some variance for cultural idiosyncrasies, and almost all who experience them recall with vivid detail and clarity, the key markers associated with a near death experience.

As far as hallucinations are concerned, Dr. Sam Parnia of the Department of Medical Specialties in the UK reviewed the work of Dr. Fenwick and concluded the following:

"NDE in cardiac arrests appear different to hallucination arising from metabolic or physiological alteration, in that they appear to occur in a non-functioning cortex. Therefore, it is difficult to apply the same arguments for their occurrence. In addition, cerebral localization studies have indicated that thought processes are mediated through a number of different cortical areas, rather than single areas of the brain. Therefore, a globally disordered brain would not be expected to produce lucid thought processes."

In addition, Dr. Fenwick points out that people tend to forget hallucinations but retain, with great and vivid detail, their experiences of NDEs. In essence, if hallucinations require the joint function of multiple points within the cerebral cortex and those areas are non-functional, it cannot be a hallucination. Additionally, when a patient recovers, they are generally unable to remember many details as to specific images of a hallucination whereas the details of a NDE, while unconscious, are clear and specific.

Perhaps the most popularized objection to NDEs is the explanation that as the brain shuts down, it follows a natural progression that resembles what old black and white television tubes did in response to the power being turned off. It creates a dynamic where all the energy of the television display merges to the center of the screen in the form of a singular dot and slowly dissipates. The resulting "tunnel effect" and the "bright light at the end" is a commonly stated experience. Although this argument appears logical, it is proven otherwise with the simultaneous recording of brain output and heart rates. After eleven seconds of the heart rate stopping, brainwaves go flat, as recorded by the electroencephalogram (EEG), and the individual slips into unconsciousness. There is no brain activity after eleven seconds and as such, there is no possibility of the brain creating structured and lucid images or having the capacity to recall any of them. This produces an interesting phenomenon in that those having NDEs, according to science, should not be able to generate, maintain or recall anything—yet this is precisely the time when NDEs occur.

Dr. Fenwick concludes that between 10%-20% of all cardiac arrest patients have NDEs. They occur during a period of unconsciousness and are not due to medication, electrolytes, or blood gases. They are frequently described in a similar manner—patients often describe separation from their physical bodies and hoovering above the room, usually on or near the ceiling, and looking down on themselves and those in that space. Some can recall conversations and specific details of events they couldn't possibly know. As an example, Dr. Fenwick recalls the story of a very pragmatic retired Army major who survived two heart attacks and who had a NDE in each of these situations. In his first experience, the major's wife, who did not show up at the hospital until after he became unconscious, was wearing a red pant suit. After his resuscitation, he discovered his wife beside him wearing the same outfit.

Dr. Fenwick cites several additional examples in his research but the most astounding from my view, is that of a young female toddler, slightly over the age of three, who experiences reflex anoxic seizures in which her heart stops. In her short life, she clinically died over twenty times. During these periods of unconsciousness, she reported out-of-body experiences. In a videotape interview of one such event, the young girl describes a scene where she is looking down from the ceiling and watching her mother attempting to resuscitate her. While recalling the series of events, the young girl becomes irritable and chides her mother for doing it, "all wrong." In the video interview the child describes the process as she goes up to the ceiling and can "see mommy helping me." During this particular episode, she was furious with her mother for not placing her on the floor as they'd been taught by the doctor. The mother explains that during seizures, "She has no vital signs; she has no respiration, no pulse, no heartbeat, no anything" but the child usually recovers within a minute and "clicks" back into her body. During the time she is legally dead and unconscious, she can view her immediate environment and hear conversations while perched in the ceiling. When she recovers the young girl is able to retain the words her mother spoke to her, as well as specific details of the event, and convey them back to her mother.

More recently, Elon Musk's company, Neuralink, has been approved for human testing and the EEG reports of three dying patients have been recorded as of this writing. The tests have shown that after the heart stops and the patient is declared dead, the brain continues to function for a brief time. The Neuralink researchers, perhaps unaware of Dr. Fenwick's prior research, were quick to declare the flare-up of brain activity after death, is the probable cause of the rampant reports of NDE's. Although the research process is in its inception, to date, it offers no significant addition to what is already known—the brain stays active eleven seconds after the heart and lungs cease to function. It does not explain how people who have NDE's twenty or thirty minutes after they are declared dead, are able to account for the vivid details of their experience. The most obvious conclusion for me is the researcher's declaration that NDEs were "rampant."

A childhood friend of mine shared the similar experience of cardiac arrest while in the back of an ambulance. He hovered above his body inside the vehicle and remembers hearing and seeing the medical personnel working on him. He was in a state of total contentment, absorbed within a light while drifting toward a figure he knew to be Jesus. The heavenly environment he appeared in was filled with images, sounds, sensations, and beauty that were completely beyond his experience or comprehension. He felt loved, secure, and content as he communicated with Jesus. Although they didn't speak with words, he completely understood the message and realized he was being given a choice to return to his body. His memory of the situation was vivid and absolutely real to him.

American novelist, Ernest Hemingway, was wounded by shrapnel during a battle along the banks of the river Piave in Italy during World War I. While recovering in Milan, he wrote a letter to his family with the cryptic statement, *"Dying is a very simple thing. I've looked at death and really, I know."*

Years later, Hemingway explained the details of his experience to a friend. *"A big Austrian trench mortar bomb, of the type that used to be called ash cans, exploded in the darkness. I felt my soul or something coming right out of my body, like you'd pull a silk handkerchief out of a pocket by one corner. It flew around and then came back and went in again and I wasn't dead anymore."*

Hemingway was deeply affected by the NDE and as with many others who share the experience, he became a softer person afterwards. In his novel, *"A Farewell to Arms,"* Hemingway portrays a character named Frederic Henry who faces death on the battlefield and the account is remarkably similar to his own.

"I ate the end of my piece of cheese and took a swallow of wine. Through the other noise I heard a cough, then came the chuh-chuh-chuh-chuh —then there was a flash, as when a blast-furnace door is swung open, and a roar that started white and went red and on and on in a rushing wind. I tried to breathe but my breath would not come, and I felt myself rush bodily out of myself and out and out and out and all the time bodily in the wind. I went out swiftly, all of myself, and I knew I was dead and that it had all been a mistake to think you just died. Then I floated, and instead of going on I felt myself slide back. I breathed and I was back."

Other well-known personalities such as Jane Seymour, George Lucas and Peter Sellers have also explained accounts of having NDEs. There's a very high probability that nearly everyone has personal knowledge of someone who has had a similar experience. As widespread as these events seem to be, they fall outside of the scope of any known scientific paradigm, thus it becomes difficult to explain without interjecting the possibility of the existence of God. As such, it requires one to either redefine the definition of consciousness or scramble to explain the incredibly accurate descriptions and vivid details provided by those having NDEs while unconscious. Some researchers have responded by expressing the view that the brain may not function as the source of our mental processes but act as a transducer of our thoughts and feelings. It's conjectured to be similar to the way a television set receives data from an outside source and converts it into a form of energy that we can see and hear. According to Dr. Melvin Morse's bold and provocative theory, there is a place in the right temporal lobe of our brain that literally communicates with God. He calls it the "God Spot."

Deathbed Phenomena/ Deathbed Visions

Throughout history, until less than a century ago, it was common for families to gather at bedside while their beloved family member passed. This was not only a display of love and devotion to the nearly departed but it was common for the terminally ill or injured to experience deathbed phenomena (DBP). Family members often sat bedside with great anticipation and expectation, perhaps secretly hoping to witness a connection to "the other side." There is nothing new in this process as the ancient Greeks wrote of these experiences, as have all who followed. The only difference today is that over the course of the previous century, the vast majority of families have become separated from what used to be the final intimate moments of a loved one's life. We are now largely disengaged from the dying process and as a result, anything that deals with death and dying seems foreign, uncomfortable and odd to us.

The language and identifying terminology that attempts to convey the meaning of near death and pre-death experiences is varied and sometimes vague. The major distinction between a NDE and deathbed phenomena (DBP) is that NDEs typically are sudden and most often experienced in a state of unconsciousness whereas deathbed phenomena or deathbed visions happen slowly and primarily to people who are dying of a progressive illness. These events can include conscious visions of angels, deceased relatives, and religious figures as well as premonitions of death or precognitive experiences in the form of dreams. Because these deathbed experiences encompass more than simply visions, it's easier to refer to them collectively as deathbed phenomena or DBPs.

According to the research statistics presented by Nurse Practitioner, April Mazzarino-Willett published in the *American Journal of Hospital and Palliative Medicine* in 2010, of the approximately 10% of terminally ill patients who remain conscious prior to their death, an astonishing 50%-60% percent experience DBP. Those who work with the terminally ill are quite familiar with DBP as 70% percent report that a patient has told them about a DBP, 72% percent report that a relative has told them about a DBP and 65% have witnessed one (Alberta Health Services, Calgary Survey).

What does a DBP look like? It can include several things, many of which seem to be the subject of late-night sci-fi programs. The most common of these events include communication with deceased relatives, friends, and angelic or religious figures. During these times, they may report seeing places of great beauty or Heaven. On more rare occasions, hospice personnel report such phenomena as changes in room temperature, changes in pet behavior, clocks stopping, bell ringing, and visions of vapors. It's difficult to confirm how "real" these instances are in research because of the social stigma associated with these events. There are, however, those who are pressing for a greater amount of investigation into these matters. Researcher, Dr. Uma MacConville, states, *"There is no rational explanation for DBP but so many have had similar experiences that it cannot be discounted."*

Dr. Fenwick includes a few examples of DBP in his lecture, one of which comes from a research paper by Paola Giovetti (1999, p. 38) that typifies 40% of DBP described as "take-away" visions. In one case, *"The gauze over his face moved, I ran to him and with his last strength he said to me: Adrianna, my dear, your mother (who died three years before) is helping me break out of this disgusting body. There is so much light here, so much peace."*

Other common deathbed visions experienced by the nearly deceased involve being taken to waiting places such as beautiful landscapes or gardens. Those in the company of one having such a vision may see their loved one's eyes widen with wonder while expressing joy in this lovely environment. It's not uncommon for them to see a room full of people, perhaps gathered for a party in anticipation of their arrival. They may or may not speak aloud while in this state and such visions may have multiple occurrences as the loving people that assist them to move on.

As a hospice chaplain, I have encountered several patients who express what I have come to refer to as "departure language." In the days, weeks—or even months prior to their deaths, patients develop a sense of urgency akin to anticipating an upcoming event. In one case, I had a patient who wanted me to look in her closet for her blue gown as it had to be ready for an upcoming gala. I had known this patient for over a year and was aware she had not been out of her bed or ventured out of her room in all that time. She went on to explain that she was going to put on her gown and go downstairs to the lobby where a handsome man was going to pick her up in a big limo and they were going to an extravagant party at the beach.

The primary caregiver and daughter-in-law of one of my patients tells this story:

My 91-year-old mother-in-law loves to garden, and when she started displaying signs of dementia, we would often spend time in the garden. During these times, she frequently looked up to the trees and smiled. When I asked her what she was smiling at, she asked, 'Do you see the beautiful women in the trees?' On other occasions, as I began to sit in a chair near her, she stated, 'Oh, don't sit there, there's someone already sitting there.' When I asked who was sitting there, she replied, 'One of the beautiful women.'"

Another patient's adult son states that his mom sees a little, cherub-looking boy sitting on a nearby pillow or on the headrest behind her. Sometimes when the son attempts to sit down, his mother cautions him to sit somewhere else as the little boy is sitting there.

A childhood friend of mine named Debbie, took the time to write down the events that occurred when her mother passed at a hospice care facility in 2012. In the weeks leading up to her admission, mom was taking heavy medications that resulted in her experiencing hallucinations that left her frustrated, frantic, and confused. Once settled into the hospice, she was taken off chemotherapy, painful injections, and the other powerful life-prolonging drugs responsible for her delusions. Almost immediately she became much more lucid and alert. During this time of greater mental clarity, her mother began to experience DBP. On one occasion, Debbie's husband entered his mother-in-law's hospice unit and greeted mom and Debbie. The two women were the only people in the room. After greeting the two, "*...mom looked around and asked who all the people were in the room with us. Then her eyes glanced away from us to the side, and she excitedly said, 'Oh, there's my brother. I want to go talk to him!'*"

This experience was much different than the hallucinations she once had while under the influence of powerful medications. When hallucinating, mom was frustrated, frantic and confused. In this new environment, she remained calm and only became excited when she saw her brother. These encounters happened many times over the course of the next couple of weeks. Sometimes she seemed to be engaged in conversation with others and other times she seemed to be listening to them and acknowledging what they were saying. Once she moved her feet over as if to allow someone to sit at the edge of her bed. When Debbie asked her about it, mom cupped her hand over her mouth and whispered, "That lady from the party wants to sit down." Soon after, she excitedly called across the room to "Thelma" and patted the bed as an invitation for Thelma to sit down next to her. She had a lengthy conversation with Thelma and judging from her hand motions, the two were sewing together. At times she included Debbie in the conversation as though Debbie could hear their dialog. Later that same day, she quickly sat up in bed and while leaning forward, used both hands to excitedly blow kisses to someone across the room. Debbie asked who the kisses were for, but mom became a little coy in the moment and said they were for her. Debbie was quick to point out that mom was blowing kisses in the opposite direction, and she responded only with silence. Later that evening she confessed, "Your dad had a twinkle in his eye tonight."

In the year that led up to her final days at the hospice, Debbie's mom was often scared and angry while experiencing dreadful hallucinations. The final two weeks of her life in hospice were characterized by whispered conversations and heavenly visitors who served to calm and prepare her to transition into her new life in eternity.

Review

Although Raymond Moody's book, *"Life After Life"* was heavily criticized after its publication in 1975, current research has validated his theories. The development and distribution of automated external defibrillator devices (AED's) have resulted in a marked increase in the number of people who normally would have died due to cardiac arrest. Many of these survivors experience near-death experiences (NDE) in which they can recall with detail the events and conversations of those while in a clinical state of death. After eleven seconds, the brain shuts down and there is no EEG activity, but this is precisely when deathbed phenomena occurs. Examples of such activities are quite normal in terminal patients as up to 60% of those not on heavy medications report experiencing them.

Things to Know

*Always review and implement the previously suggested, "Things to Know" and "Things to Do" from the earlier chapters. Continue to add to your story. Keep writing, making notes and dating them.

1. Science and theology are not necessarily adversaries. Throughout history both fields of study have been adjusted as new data is discovered. In my view, God created science and all science eventually points back to God.
2. In *"Mourning and Melancholia"* (1917), Freud suggested that mourners had to reclaim energy that they had invested in the deceased loved one. Relationships take up energy; letting go of them, psychiatrists theorize, entails mental work. When you lose someone close to you, have to reassess your picture of the world and your place in it.
3. *"Bad grief has many faces of which denial, busyness and wallowing alone in self-pity are three common expressions. Additionally, grief is not an emotion that one can overcome by simply thinking positive thoughts. Although a positive attitude is a*

wonderful attribute, if it's utilized as a form of denial, it's simply masking the real issue by bandaging a wound that hasn't been properly treated. Bad grief utilizes work, activity, food, alcohol, social activities and helping others as a distraction or avoidance mechanism. It all serves as a means to evade vulnerability. It's simply the lid to a box that one doesn't want to peer into for fear that the box will inescapably encase them. Bad grief is isolation, unexpressed anger, and fear." —Unknown

Things to Do

1. Ask family members or close friends if they know of anyone who has experienced a NDE or Deathbed Phenomena. You may be surprised to discover how common the experience is even though few openly speak of it.
2. Volunteer with a local hospice organization. Sit bedside with those who are experiencing the transition of life—listen to their life histories, and provide comfort and friendship.
3. Make final arrangements for your family prior to a state of urgency. It's much easier to discuss and put in place such things as wills, estate planning, final arrangements, durable power of attorney for medical and other matters prior to an emergency.

Depend upon it, your dying hour will be the best hour you have ever known! Your last moment will be your richest moment, better than the day of your birth will be the day of your death. It shall be the beginning of heaven, the rising of a sun that shall go no more down forever!

— C.H. Spurgeon

Chapter 12
Where We Go From Here

An Artist's View

I was listening to an interview with a well-known artist, and he was asked how he examined a painting. The seasoned artist offered an insightful explanation: he first looked at a painting from three inches away so he could see the fine brush strokes and minuscule details. He then stood back approximately three feet from the canvass and viewed the subject of the painting, observing the use of light, hue, and texture. Finally, he stepped away from the painting ten to twenty feet. From this vantage point, he could see the whole composition from beginning to end while absorbing the entirety of the context, scope, and message of the work.

When we first engage with loss, our noses are only inches from the canvas of our loved one's life, and we are keenly aware of our grief. Our faces are so deeply absorbed by this close-up view, nothing else seems to exist around us. As we begin to process our emotions and come to terms with what's happening, we are gradually able to take small steps back. From a few feet away, the view is much different. The perspective with a larger vantage point allows us to see and appreciate the broader view of our loved one's life. We can see and value the intricate color changes and how they all blend to form this image of who we love. A few more steps back and we're able to view the grand scheme of the person's life from beginning to end, the time they were in our lives and now the beautiful representation left behind for us to remember them. This is how we process grief. It's a transition of perspective, a gradual reorientation. We never lose our loved one's value to us, we simply learn to view them differently.

Our View

Have you ever gone through an ugly duckling stage in life? Mine was in the eighth grade. Growing up in San Diego, the cool look for a kid my age was to have long, straight hair, combed so that it produced an angular bang that swooped across the forehead—the surfer look. In obvious defiance to the style of the day, I was a chubby little kid with curly hair, acne, small ears, and a missing tooth. I'm not sure I even measured up to ugly duck standards. A new category had to be created to describe the way I looked.

Dad wouldn't allow me to grow my hair long, and we were poor so the missing front tooth I knocked out on the playground in the fifth grade was never fixed. The teeth that remained shifted over into the empty space, creating somewhat of a shark-like smile. This created a problem for me on the day school pictures were taken. Because of my embarrassing smile, I either feigned illness or smiled without displaying my teeth. Mom didn't like the toothless smiles so she made me promise I would smile for my eighth-grade picture. After some deliberation, I reluctantly agreed to do it for her. She completed the order form, purchasing the deluxe package with eighty gazillion copies so everyone we ever knew, and future generations could have one.

The day of the photo we were instructed to wear something colorful, so I wore my favorite red shirt. As fate would have it, that same morning I had a huge acne outbreak and I looked like I barely survived an African bee attack. Being a kid, I didn't realize that my red shirt accentuated the acne, further intensifying the breakout and the redness of my face.

If that were not enough, my hair was short and curly. My hair doesn't do the long, straight, surfer look very well. The slightest imbalance in humidity, perspiration or physical activity would send my little repressed curls straight up into little pigtail-type spirals from my skull. I had hoped our photos would be taken in the morning when my little curls were more obedient, but destiny demanded they be taken in the afternoon, immediately following my physical education class. By this time, all I had to offer the camera were greasy little curls that shot up at random from my head.

I sat in front of the camera, terrified. I promised mom I would smile so I forced myself to open my mouth and show off all my crooked pearly whites. Unfortunately, rather than a smile, it resembled something more akin to an expression one might have when they must use the restroom really, really badly and the nearest potty is really, really far away. It was a painful, hopeless expression perhaps only witnessed here and on the faces of convicted criminals. In the end, I looked like a desperate soul trapped inside a burning pineapple. The shirt looked great though.

Mom sent out photos to everyone we knew or were related to, and the calls started coming in. "I didn't know you had a special needs child, Ms. Keebler."

Mom replied, "Oh, he's normal. He looks like that all the time,"

After a brief pause the caller stated, "That sure is a pretty shirt."

I destroyed as many of the pictures as I could find but little brother has a devious soul and smelled an opportunity. By the ninth grade I had grown six or seven inches in height, lost all my baby fat, had braces put on my teeth, the acne disappeared, and hair styles changed. I was more athletic, so my pudgy little body had become more appealing, and I started dating girls. Unfortunately, each time I had a new girlfriend, guess who showed up to offer them a copy of my eighth-grade picture? Yes, little brother. I thought I had destroyed all of them, but he hid them in different places and just when I thought I had removed the last of them, he came up with another one. He plagued me up until my senior year in college. I'm pretty sure I destroyed them all by now, but mom did send out quite a few to relatives. I pray they have been lost or destroyed because the flaming pineapple needs to rest in peace forever. I used to tell people that we kept the photos under the kitchen sink to scare bugs away.

My experience is not that unusual. Christian writer, A.W. Tozer, tells a story of a young woman who came to his office for counseling. He describes her as one of the most beautiful women he had ever met. After she sat down and cried for a moment, he gently asked the woman why she came to see him. "I'm just so ugly! I don't know what to do."

Although Tozer was shocked, he questioned her as to why she thought this about herself and was able to trace it back to her life in eighth grade. She was a tall, lanky girl with big feet and one of the popular boys referred to her appearance as being like a duck. She retained that image in her mind to the present day. Over the years she has received thousands of compliments attesting to her beauty but would not accept the truth of the statements. Tozer described the dynamic as being like a person tuning a radio and hearing only static. The beautiful woman filtered out all the compliments she received over the years because she would not allow herself to believe otherwise.

Grief works in a similar manner. It distorts how we think and act, how we perceive ourselves and even our capabilities. Grief has the power to dwarf every asset and attribute we possess. It's not a place where we want to get stuck. How do we get out from under this weight? Begin by acknowledging who you were before you lost your loved one. You haven't lost any of these qualities. They may be weakened for a short time and that's normal, but you will regain your sense of self identity. Furthermore, this horrible experience over time will add to your list of attributes. Once you step away from the static, you'll emerge stronger, more sensitive to other's needs and much more aware of priorities and passions. We are not that ugly eighth grader. We have grown, been equipped with knowledge, have a direction, and are aware of the pitfalls of grief along the way. We need only to focus on our strengths, surround ourselves with people who are encouraging and who believe in us, and trust God to keep and protect our hearts.

My Name in Africa

My short-term missionary trips to Africa are among the most memorable and fulfilling adventures of my life. On one of these journeys, our small team, comprised of three Americans and three Africans, joined together at a missionary compound located in Nairobi, Kenya. Although I was familiar with the two Americans, I was meeting the Africans for the first time. Nobby, a tall and lean man whose grin seemed to cover his entire face, was a brilliant local pastor from Kenya. Rose, also from Kenya, was a songbird and worship leader that seemed to possess the ability to call down angels from on high when she led our worship services. Jessica, the final member of the trio, was from Uganda and was a gifted teacher and public speaker.

From Nairobi, our team flew into Kenya's second largest city of Kakamega and from there we trekked into the small, remote villages that dappled the countryside. Although tribes speak with their regional dialects, English is the official national language of Kenya and all the children that attend school are required to learn it. Often, when we approach a village, the children are the first to come out and greet us. I learned to sit down in an open space and let them gather in a circle around me. The children are beautiful. They giggle and laugh because I am very likely, the first Caucasian person they have ever seen. I am actually mixed race, primarily Native American and German, but my olive skin is far lighter than anything they have ever been exposed to. I already know from experience that they are curious and want to touch my skin but it's a bit of a game as to how we arrive at that point. Most often one of the older children will ask in a very polite manner, speaking to me in Oxford English with a charming accent. I extend my arm and they are somewhat tentative at first, slowly touching me and then immediately examining their fingers to see if my white had rubbed off on them. After seeing the first child survive, the others are eager to join in. The children seem a little surprised that my skin is much like their own. Some of the boys will display their bravado by not only touching me but holding onto my arm as though they were risking a high charge of electricity. This only works until the inevitable happens—another child will come up from behind, placing their fingers firmly into the side of the first child and scaring them. Their temporary bravery is dispelled but the laughter that ensues is contagious.

On one occasion a larger child pushed a small child from behind, nearly forcing him onto my lap. The smaller child's eyes widened with fear as my alien hands reached out to help prevent him from falling. As I touched the little boy, there was a pregnant hush, and then when the circle of children realized he was not going to die, they all erupted with laughter. After we spent a few moments becoming acquainted, I passed out gum to the children and took their photographs. They had never seen an image of themselves so seeing their image on the viewfinder was almost magical to them. It was a fun experience for everyone.

Once inside the village or small community, our days were filled with activities such as praying for the sick, meeting with village elders, visiting schools and orphanages and teaching. In the early evening we often conducted services or offered training. By the end of a very long day, our team members were tired and ready to relax. When we returned to our rooms each evening, we enjoyed gathering, telling stories, and laughing among ourselves. Nobby was my roommate for the trip. He was often amused by me, and his infectious laugh prompted me to become more comedic than normal. Our room seemed to always generate a lot of good stories and laughs so it was common for all our team to gather with us before heading off to sleep.

As a footnote, I must interject that Africans from larger communities are very familiar with American television programs—especially the old shows of the '60's and 70's. They are also familiar with the American commercials and the slang expressions from the ads.

Having this as background, one night while the team was gathered in our room, I walked past a mirror. Glancing into it, I could see that everyone was watching me, so I paused to gaze at my reflection in the mirror. With everyone's eyes on me, I quickly turned, flipping my imaginary long hair away from my face while imitating the famous commercial where the gorgeous model, Kelly LeBrock, flips her long dark hair away from her face and states, "Don't hate me because I'm beautiful." We all had a good laugh, probably the best one of the evening.

The following morning the team gathered at breakfast as was our normal routine. Nobby was reading from a list of our day's upcoming activities and recited each of our names in relation to what our task was for the day. When he read my name, he stated both my first and last name: Edward Keebler. Upon hearing my full name our team member form Uganda, Jessica, began to laugh very hard. The rest of us paused to look at her and then I looked at the Kenyans to see if I missed a cultural idiosyncrasy. They shrugged their shoulders at me and shook their heads. They had no idea why she was laughing. After Jessica calmed down, Nobby continued reading off the list of tasks for the day and who would be responsible for whatever task. He came to my name again and read it aloud. Jessica doubled up with laughter once again. When her laughter began to subside, we asked her what was so funny. She said it was my last name. Looking around the table at all our blank stares, she demanded, "What is Edward's real last name?" Nobby repeated my last name, and she held back from laughing until finally becoming a little agitated and claimed we were all trying to play a trick on her. There was an extended pause as she evaluated the sincerity of our expressions. Satisfied that we were not playing a trick on her, she looked up and said, "In Uganda, that is similar to a word for beautiful."

When an outsider comes to Africa and is accepted into African culture, they assign that person a new name. From this day onward, my name in Africa is "Beautiful." Whenever any of my African friends send me an email, the opening line is often, "Hello Beautiful, how are you?"

In the years that have followed, I began to suspect that Jessica's interpretation of my name was not accurate. I checked all the local tribal dialects for the word, "beautiful" and no word appears to fit. I suspect that the Africans, being such a polite and encouraging people, did not want to cause me embarrassment or shame, so she created the interpretation up on the spot. It is much more likely that her outburst of laughter resulted in her exposure to the old Keebler Cookie commercials, and she thought everyone was teasing me with a Keebler Elf reference. Regardless of the situation and the accuracy of the word, my African friends gave me the name "Beautiful" and I'm going to keep it.

When we examine how God views us, it's entirely different than the way we see ourselves. We tend to define our lives in terms of our failures, and grief exacerbates that perspective. God, in contrast, views us through the lens of our victories. For example, on the errant side of King David's life, we see him as an adulterer and murderer, but from a heavenly perspective, he is known as "a man after God's heart." There are many examples of fallible followers of God who lived less than perfect lives, but God changed their names. They continued to be imperfect, but their lives took on added depth and meaning. Each time someone's name was changed, it served to clear the static of an "ugly duck" past or self-perception and provided a view of who they were in God's eyes.

In ancient Greece a white stone represented acquittal of the one being tried. White stones were also used as tokens for admission or membership to public festivals. In Revelation 2:17 a white stone with a new name is given to those that overcome. Although there are different perspectives as to what the name is referring to, I think a plausible interpretation is that we are given a new name in eternity. We will no longer be bound and defined by the failures of our flesh but given a name that reflects our true value in God's eyes.

As we progress through grief, our eyes will gradually move farther away from the canvas of our lost loved one and we will begin to view their lives on a larger scale. Up to this point, the intimacy of our lives has been so integrated with theirs, we cannot tell which brush stokes belong to them and which are our own. We, begrudgingly, must step away to see the beauty of their life apart from us, and discover who we are apart from them. This action causes a tearing of our heart, mind, and soul. It challenges our view of ourselves as we are left feeling wounded and incomplete by the loss. It is at this time that we must align our thoughts of self with the way God views us. It's not easy and it takes time, but that's the direction we must move. Taking small steps in the right direction leads us to a place where we begin to see ourselves as God sees us... beauty in imperfection.

Review

Having finished the book, you are ready to start the work of grief. Processing grief is not something you can rush but it is productive to exert effort in a positive direction. Realize, failure is part of the process. What part does God play in your story? Many people get stuck in grief on the first question. If you're angry with God, be angry. Express any emotion you feel toward God as He can handle your thoughts and feelings on any level. Why God? Why did you allow this life to be taken? The theological answer is simple but in circumstances such as this, not immediately consoling. Sin came into the world through the disobedience of humanity. Love requires a choice and when we chose to disobey God, the consequences of sin entered our world. We all die, but for what purpose? Why now? We will likely never know why our loved one died. We can only know that there is a plan for the redemption of humanity through the death, burial, and resurrection of Christ. We take refuge in the fact that Jesus overcame death, hell and the grave and where He is, we will also be. The Apostle Paul wrote that we do not grieve like those outside the church because we have the blessed hope of the resurrection of Christ.

Often in grief, it seems as though God is far away from us. It's difficult to hear His voice as pain can block His presence. But God speaks to us in grief and sometimes that's through dreams. Dreams can provide direction, inspire and warn but dreams should always be filtered by scripture and wise counsel.

As we begin to process grief, initially we're going to feel numb, as though nothing is real. Once we escape from the fog of grief, everything is disorganized but in time, we're able to put things back in place, only in a different arrangement. William Worden explains that we have four tasks to complete along the way and that's to acknowledge the death of your loved one, express the emotions of grief, adapt to a new life, and relocate precious memories by releasing the tears in favor of the joy of a shared life. Having the overall view of the grief landscape, we develop a plan and establish a new direction by following an established route as illustrated in the story of the church softball team.

Along the way, we're going to face obstacles and we must be mindful of them, or we risk becoming "stuck" in grief or subject to complicated or prolonged grief. Working through grief involves understanding the process, taking on the pain, and forgiving others. The difficult part of forgiveness is applying it to our own lives in the form of self-forgiveness. Some of us have deep emotional wounds that are exacerbated by grief, and we must take time to recognize, forgive, and protect our hearts. Sometimes that means loving at an arm's length in abusive relationships.

We will undoubtedly face some failures along the way. We sometimes make decisions or enter relationships too soon, and other times we're pressured into doing things we're not comfortable with. Some of the major obstacles we face are identified by the acronym FAIL: Fear, Anger, Isolation and Lethargy. In the process of adapting to a new life, we must be conscious of "triggers" or situations, events and things that jolt us back into the initial pain of grief, and prepare for them.

Others have been where you are, and have successfully traversed the path of grief. The failures and victories of some of those who attended my class are reflected in their personal stories. As added assurance of an afterlife, there are the personal stories of some of my own experiences along with former patients and childhood friends as they experienced deathbed phenomena. Despite some who label this data as "paranormal," it is biblically supported and scientifically sound.

Finally, we initially see the person for whom we are grieving with our nose close to the canvas of their lives. We are familiar with the fine brush strokes and details of their lives but as we progress through the grieving process, we take steps back, not to be dismissive of their lives, but to appreciate them from a different perspective. As we step back, we become more aware of the larger scope of their life while becoming more aware of our individual self. Grief convinces us we're ugly and lack value. God views us in terms of our victories and inner beauty.

Things to Do

The success of your journey of grief utilizing my methodology highly depends on your participation in the process. As previously stated, I want you to write your story of grief—record your struggles, growth, and failures. Granted, not everyone is a writer but almost anyone can jot down bullet points or make notations of their thoughts and feelings. Those who are disabled can achieve the same end with a voice recording. To help with the writing process, I have the *Comfort in Grief Workbook* that will provide more detailed instructions and guidance.

Once you've made notations on each topic and dated the entries, the process is far from over. This is just the starting point—a sort of "You Are Here" indication as you're examining a map of the process. Those who journal or are willing to start, plan to have pen and paper in hand to record an inspiring thought, trigger, or struggle—and make sure to date it. This project will take at least a year to complete, two years is even better but don't be distracted by time. Along the way, and especially at the end, you'll be able to look back with astonishment at your growth.

> *"Beyond our most stubborn misperception lies often our fondest dream."*

> — Robert Breault

Closing Remarks

I am sorry for your loss, dear reader. In these closing lines my hope is that in this journey, we have shared some laughter and tears together, that we have been inspired and learned how to process our loss. I cannot see your face but in prayerful meditation I have imagined you reading this book and I pray that the Holy Spirit will comfort your heart and lovingly guide you through this place in life. I have been where you are and am able to state with confidence that it is possible to recover from tragic loss. It is within our grasp to once again, live a happy and content life. We can step away from fear and love again, recover an appreciation of the beauty in the world and experience the wonderment of life anew. It begins with a series of small steps and a willing heart. My prayer is that my message and experiences will serve as a faithful guide for you to follow.

Your fellow traveler,

Edward Keebler